AF391707

John Hicton
Philippe Saguey

THE MAN

IN THE

CAVE

A journey of self-awareness

Vol.1
52 sessions 2022

Legal notices

Self-publishing

John HICTON / Philippe SAGUEY
Impasse des côtes, 24250 La Roque-Gageac
France

Copyright 2023 - John HICTON / Philippe SAGUEY

Legal deposit 02/2023
Ed.3: 12/2025 - Layout refinement

ISBN 978-2-9586270-3-4

Price: 18€

Acknowledgments: Pat SEEDS

Introduction by John

Throughout human history man's fascination with God has been relentless. The same can be said for his fascination with science and technology. Is it possible that they could be the exact same thing?

I am not a scientist. In fact, I am not an academic of any type. All of my personal life experiences, of which I have many, are taken from my personal practical application of life, often feet first without much thought or care and attention given before I threw myself into whatever I felt like doing in that given moment. Sometimes, it was an incredible experience; often, it was not.

I have always had an interest in all that life could offer me, be that socially or in a learned self-taught and self-applied respect. But I have always asked myself the question, "What is the real meaning of life?"

I have waltzed through life not really knowing what I want from it. Often I met people in my life who achieved a specific career, like a doctor, and they have declared to me that from a small child this was what they had always wanted to do. Well, I'm not that, not that this is a bad thing. As you carry on reading, you will learn that there is no such thing as a bad thing in the context that you are conditioned to understand it. Some people just seem to know what they must do. I never did.

There is no such thing as a coincidence, and there exists a defined pattern to everything that occurs in your life. So I can only conclude that if you are here, then there is a reason for you being here. If you have started to read this book, then I would suggest that there is a defined reason for you being in this space, here and now. I don't know the reason, but I would certainly think there is a reason, and you might already know what that reason is.

This book is based on a series of meditations that took place in the year of 2022. They were conducted by myself and my friend and neighbour Philippe. The meditations soon took on the form of channeling, myself as the antenna—something I had never experienced before. The venue for these meditations was a cave next to Philippe's home. The meditations were audio recorded and then transcribed to text.

I have contemplated many times what to call these meditations. I do not believe they are lessons. I believe that they are a guidebook to the understanding of what is God. They are an explanatory to a layperson like myself as to how it all works, the answer to the meaning of life, the questions that I have continually asked myself all my life.

The sessions are written exactly as they were spoken, and each session in the cave lasted between 30 to 45 minutes.

The entity channeling through me does not give a name or title, neither does he refer to us with a name or a title. He merely calls us energy. When you read the sessions, you will understand why. Philippe and I did, however, due to the fact we had very long and deep discussions around the meditations, refer to his or her energy as «The Man In The Cave». For this book, I will refer to the meditations as sessions.

My introduction is intentionally small. The sessions make up most of the content. I do not want to influence your opinion in any way as to what you are about to read.

However, I will end this book with my own comments. This will be my own and short conclusion based on what I have listened to in the cave. Yours may be different.

<u>Introduction by Philippe</u>

I quickly sensed that an incredible phenomenon was developing during our meditations. It was no longer John expressing some ideas but a third party taking an active part in our sessions! The choice of words, without the slightest hesitation, the intonation, this tone of voice, this fantastic metaphysical information, but also this proximity, since the entity which spoke through John's mouth was also speaking directly to us... Our meditations had just taken an extraordinary turn! And we began to record them...

I have studied for many years the phenomenon and teachings of Seth, a non-physical entity considered by most of today's great explorers of consciousness to be the greatest modern metaphysical teacher. Channelled by the medium Jane Roberts in the USA in the 1970s and 1980s, he gave rise to the New Age movement. I was stunned at the thought of having a similar live experience!

It is remarkable that John, without ever having heard of Seth, has an innate knowledge of his main theories. I myself have only an 'intellectual' knowledge of them and a very incomplete one. In other words, I want to believe in it; and I do. John doesn't have to believe in it; he knows!

This illustrates a kind of complicity, convergence, complementarity perhaps between John and me. Despite our very different backgrounds, there is a deep connection between us that is difficult to explain. We understand each other. Even if I believed in coincidences, by what chance could I have moved into the house next door? And why this deep desire to improve my English for a few years? And that cave in the garden... The Man In The Cave, as it will be called, will soon give us explanations...

Anyway, it seemed written that we would have to share an experience. I didn't know it would be exceptional!

<u>Session 1 - 10/04/2022</u>

The path you choose to take is derived in this realm through an emotional action, an emotional decision, an emotional reaction. It is not the same everywhere else, only here. If you apply logic to your decision, it's correct. But logic is merely a tool that exists here. Everything you see, everything you hear, everything you smell, everything you touch has an effect on your direction because it affects your emotion. Your choices are made through, through these directions. There's no wrong way to go and there's no right way to go; you will go. You have so many more senses, so many more skills that you are not even aware of. You accept an emotion to create a reaction. If you don't accept the emotion, you create a different reaction. You choose. You choose here. You choose everywhere.

Do not apportion blame for your choices. Do not blame something else or somebody else. It's your choice. You have total freedom to choose what you want to accept and what you don't want to accept. You might feel that you don't have a choice, but you do, always. To be able to discern the information you get is a skill. You need to learn because your actions will be based on that information, and your actions will create a reaction, a chain of events. If you don't wish to control the information, that's not a problem. It's just another way of living. You have experienced this all before; this is not new to you. You have chosen to experience it again.

You are looking constantly for someone or something to tell you what to do, to give you direction. The only direction that I can give you is to tell you to take your own counsel, take your own direction. It is not for me to tell you where to go and what to do. It's for you to know. Since here you are affected by everything, everything you see has an effect on your life. You hear, you smell, it all has an effect on your life, on your direction, on your reaction. It's for you to manage that, direct that. Colours and sounds, every little thing you see and do will have an effect on your life.

When you pray for direction, you are praying to yourself. When you ask a question, you are asking yourself, your higher self. You are totally responsible for the outcome. You cannot apportion blame. There is no blame; it doesn't exist. There is no judgement. You must take full responsibility for your actions, your own thoughts, your own creation. Learn how to manage this properly, and your world will be a different place.

You have chosen to think as one. You have chosen a difficult path, a confusing path. When you join the source again, you will know how difficult a path you have chosen. Follow your guidance, your own guidance. It is correct.

There are many worlds, many dimensions, many species, what you call ET. But it matters not. There is only one source. There is only one source, but this shouldn't concern you. There is a universal code, chaos among organisation, a bizarre appeal. Simple and yet complicated. It is the same thing.

Recognise your own fears. Turn them into an advantage, an experience. Recognise that they are but an experience. Don't keep asking for help; recognise that it is you that are going to help yourself. You know how. Look inwardly; within you lies the answers to your questions, within yourself.

You dwell in a machine that dwells on a machine. You have created this. You chose it.

<u>Session 2 - 21/04/2022</u>

Your mind throws out so many possibilities. Often this is confusing for you. You can't discern between the different possibilities you have created. This is the path you have chosen, but a uniformed pattern exists within this, although it seems it doesn't to you.

You are taught to believe that it's one way when in fact it's the complete opposite. Your conditioning will prevent your development; it will hinder it; it will slow it down. You have to learn how to separate the two. You have to learn how to apply, apply one against the other. It's a positive and a negative. You have the capability to do this. You will always be drawn back to your conditioning as a safety zone, a safety net. Your own insecurity will bring you back time and time again to your conditioning, your own fear. You will repeat this process many times until you are fully aware it is but a process.

Persevere, experience. Emotions are energy, frequencies are energy. They can be applied however you choose to apply them or however you don't choose to apply them. Very few are aware of this in the realm that you exist in. Do not fear for the future, it is pointless. It is a relentless exercise and a pointless exercise. The future is already written. There are less than you think.

You are in one world of which there are many, one process of many processes. You choose. Dig deep for your answers for they lie within you. So many distractions, you are hearing what you want to hear; you are hearing what you need to hear. There is no point to go into extensive detail of quantum physics, atomy and things that will only confuse you. It is much simpler than that for you. Learn how your emotional state is driven, how it's created, how it has a cause and effect on everything, its origin, its reason.

There is no point trying to run before you walk. Your desire to know everything can hinder you. It is a stage-by-stage process, but there is no question that cannot be answered. All the answers lie within.

Do not pay so much attention to what is occurring now in this realm. It is part of the same thing, but only a part, a small part, a small part of your potential. What you think has enormous importance really is insignificant. You interpret this with your mind. You have to step out of your mind and feel the emotion, know what it is. Understand the energy it creates; understand what to do with that energy, how to direct it, how to manipulate it. It is really not as complicated as you think it is.

Your mind will create many distractions for you. It has been designed that way. Try and understand yourself more, more than you understand others. You have a skill that you can understand others *(1)*, but it's not important to understand others; it's important to understand yourself. They are the same; it is the same thing.

You would say faith can move mountains. It surely can. It can also create them.

Remember, you are not unusual; you are not different than anybody else. Being aware is not different. They are all the same. Your realisation of that is what is important. That is awareness. Many are not aware. It doesn't mean they don't possess their inner wisdom; they just don't know how to access it. They don't even know where it is. Their soul is of an equal measure as is yours.

You asked me where I am from. I am from the same place as you, as we all are. There is only one source. When you are asking the questions, I am answering the questions. That's the reason I am here. Ask with sincerity, and anyone can get the answers. How many are asking? Not as many as you think. They are not lost; they merely don't ask. It's not as complicated as you think it is.

.... *(Transcript from audio impossible)* your conditioned imagination, you have a highly formed imagination which is often confusing for you. Exaggerated and distorted, confusing. Try not to enter this position. You have to control your ego, and don't allow your ego to control you. This is really basic, basic understanding. There is much more.

Do not unlock your Pandora's Box and unleash it on the world, and think that you have no consequences from these actions. It's common sense. But there is no good, and there is no bad; there only is.

Remember, this is only experience.

Note:
1. *John has always had this ability to experience the emotion felt by people and therefore, to understand them.*

Session 3 - 23/04/2022

I have said to you many times that you already know the answer. When you look into the soul of a person you already know the answer.

You have to ask yourself, what is your interpretation of faith? How do you perceive faith? You are not wrong to question. It is the question that will ignite your research. The questions will drive you, but there is a point of knowing. Your conditioning will always pull you back.

The very essence of what you are trying to achieve lies in your thoughts. Your thoughts are irrational; they run at tangents, this way, that way, so many thoughts. This is where your confusion lies. But knowing is much deeper, much stronger, and you do know.

There are no coincidences. Nothing happened by what you would term an accident. It may seem that way, but it is not. It is created from you, from your thoughts. How many times are you going to ask yourself, is this real? I am not going to tell you that it is real. I am going to tell you to know it is real. It is not for me to tell you it is real *(1)*. I think, so therefore, I am. You learnt that many years ago.

What is happening in these times has little relevance to your journey other than it is a driver, a force of energy that is propelling you into a different place which is infinite. In your journey, infinity is something you don't understand. It is timeless in your journey. Time is something you don't understand, but you will.

All emotions have a reason, a reason to exist. Even what you consider to be bad emotions have a reason. There is no bad, a driving force of energy.

The connection is good; it has to be pure.

You put so much emphasis on the short time you are here. It's really not so significant. A machine on a machine, you are within that machine. You chose.

The changes that are occurring now in this world have been set for a very long time, in what you call time. They have been written about many times. They are necessary. There is no deviation from this. There are no saviours. You are your saviour, if you want to use the word saviour. There are no easy ways out for you. You chose. Relax, enjoy the process. You did it many times before. Do not challenge them, it is not necessary. It is your ego. Do not fight it; it is not necessary to fight. It is your ego. What is occurring is correct. This is your experience. You will learn that your ego is just another tool. You will learn to utilise it. You will learn how to separate it from you, and to call upon it when you need it.

You are formed energy; it's the only way I can explain it to you. You are formed from energy. You are not a material being. You choose to live in this machine. It's a biological machine. You choose to dwell within it, to experience your life within it. In what you call time, it is a split second.

Just like atoms behave irrationally, or you believe they behave irrationally, it's the same for you. You are energy, and you also behave irrationally with your energy. But there is a defined uniform to this. It is something I cannot explain to you; you will never understand how this works. Your scientists are beginning to understand this. They are deliberately raising the vibration. They are trying to control it. They are limited but successful. It is of no concern to you. You will experience it soon enough. It will just confuse you to try and understand it.

There is no point for me to advise you on your conditioned life; you know the answer. Why would I do that? You already know the answers. It would be like talking to a child. There is nothing to fear. You know what is right for you.

Yes, it's very beautiful *(2)*.

Notes:
1. *We think he is talking about our sessions.*
2. *John sees a lot of images during meditations.*

Session 4 - 24/04/2022

We are all the same. You choose to live outside of the source as I do, as so too does Seth *(1)*. We are all from the same source, as one, as all.

Words are your creation, your form of communication.

There are things I don't know. There are questions I cannot answer. But we are all connected. You can be anywhere you like, in any time. What you consider time to be is different than what time really is, and you can be anywhere you like in any time you like. You choose.

You ask many questions that in reality are not logical to the world you are trying to understand. In this world it is not a question of right or wrong; it is a question of knowing. You do not have to ask the question, is it right or is it wrong? It is automatic that you know. This is much different than the world you have placed yourself in. In this world it is not difficult to access the information, it is already within you. There is no question of its authenticity.

The connection to another energy source is not difficult, but communication is often difficult in the way you would interrupt the language. The communication is difficult because the energy is different.

So yes, I do know Seth as you do *(2)*. You will choose to remember when your time, a word I don't like to use, when your time is correct, you will choose to remember.

You must always remember cause and effect within the world you live in as a species. You already know how this works. No need to ask me; you already know. You may find specific situations that you are involved in here complicated. They are not. They are simplistic. They create energy, plus and minus. In this world a balance is necessary. Too much energy one way will create what you term sadness, too much energy the other way, and you will have no understanding of anything. Both are correct. A balance is absolutely necessary. What you see occurring now in this world is a universal power, a coming together of energy, an accumulative power from people. But one is the same as the many. No winners, no losers.

In a mental form there is no necessity to eat; there is no necessity for money; there is no necessity for all the things that you value so dearly in the world you created. It is what you would term free; it's all free. There is no confusion. Such importance, you put so much importance and so much emphasis on these things, things. You do this for a reason. You create such chaos whilst you couldn't imagine the complexities of this world. You create so much chaos within your world, but the complexities are really very simple. What you perceive to be complex is not; what you perceive to be simple is complicated. For me, unnecessary.

So you see, to think as though you were in my world, for you is incredibly difficult, and for me to explain it to you is also difficult, but you have all the answers inside. Yes, I can tell you what you already know; I can remind you what you already know, but I don't think this is my place to do this. It's for you to know, to remember, more importantly to experience, to use your energy. You are your energy.

I am holding your hand as though you are a child *(3)*, that's all, to give you the comfort of knowing that there is much more within that will be projected outside of yourself. You are already aware of this.

It is not a game in the way that you interpret it as a game. But true laughter is a very positive or plus form of energy. If you are going to laugh and expend this type of energy, then you must laugh at yourself. You must always try to laugh at yourself. This will suppress your ego. Do not laugh at the misfortunes of others. Help them; this will accelerate your growth. When you help them, you are helping yourself.

Do not fear what is happening; it is necessary, necessary for all.

Do not smother your love on your family. This is not love. It will hinder them. It doesn't mean you don't love them. Allow them to grow; allow yourself to grow. You are afraid; you are afraid to make your choices. Do not protect your family until the point that you imprison them. Allow them to fly like you fly, to experience *(4)*.

The connection is good.

There are many species, many worlds of what you call ET. You are protected from these worlds. It's what you think it is; it's what you have learnt *(5)*. No need to be frightened.

<u>*Notes:*</u>
1. *Whilst the sessions seem to produce answers to questions that both John and I were subconsciously asking every day, we attempted an experiment of proof. Before starting to meditate, John told me: «Ask a question in your head, and we'll see!». So I asked The Man In The Cave this question in my head: «Do you know Seth?». I specify that we did not talk about Seth before this session.*
2. *He is obviously speaking to me, but John probably knows him. Is it possible that each of us knows him?*
3. *At this moment, John is visualising a 'Little Grey', associated with a rather unpleasant sensation. This 'Little Grey' seemed lost. John kindly asked him to get out... Could it be the 'Little Grey' who holds John's hand who is speaking to us? We don't know who or what we are dealing with yet, and need to keep our guard up...*

4. *John's wife, Tina, and I, have this instinct of over-protection…*
5. *John was not versed in the subject of aliens until I told him about the teachings of the New Message, channeled by Marshall Vian Summers. Therefore, this information seemed to be for me. And I invite the reader to read the reports entitled "The Allies of Humanity", available online free of charge on the alliesofhumanity.org website.*

Session 5 - 26/04/2022

Information you receive comes from within. You would term it data. Your data within is infinite. It is important how you manage that data, how you deal with it, how you interpret it.

I am you, and you are I *(1)*.

There is nothing to understand about ET that you don't understand about yourself; they are the same. Your curiosity will send you in many directions. Understand one and you will understand the other.

It is not my intention to confuse; it is not my intention to control, merely to inform, to remind you. You will see all of creation as a big confusing situation. It is not. It is simple. It is your own creation to do with it as you please. Your excitement will often pass your reasoning.

A crossroads, a cross is significant in these times, a symbolic cross.

You cannot fail. There is no such meaning as failure. What you determine as failure is only in your world. No winners, no losers. No right, no wrong way to go. I keep saying this; you must listen. You are uneasy… I know. You are fighting two different corners, it is correct. There is only one that is pure, but all are necessary.

Science is much different in your world than it was. You would say that scientists have learned to think outside of the box, your words. They have. Thinking with the mind is not thinking with the soul, your consciousness. Their thoughts are correct; their conclusion is not. They have little awareness of consciousness, little understanding of it.

The only limitations you put on yourself, these are your limitations. You gauge yourself; you judge yourself; you stop yourself. You allow others to influence your decisions. Why would you do that? Ask yourself, why you would do that, when you know the answer—you always know the answer— but you still allow it to happen, why? In the same way, you cannot judge others, or limit them, or control them; they too are like you. There are no limits to your ability. You limit yourself.

Everything you have created is necessary for you. All the cogs in the machine you have created are necessary for you. It is your machine. It is no one else's machine.

All energy is emotional energy. It is a driving force. Learn how to control it, how to direct it—I told you this before—and you will see what happens. You will feel what happens as will everything you have created around you feel and see the same. It is only yourself that will stop this.

When you consciously know that you chose what you chose, you will know; you will know much more. Realisation of such will free you. You won't have to ask what freedom means; you will know; you will feel it. You are not free; you are not even slightly free. Your journey has only just begun, so much to experience. Do not make it complicated for yourself. Understand the energy and the forces at work. Understand what they are, how they work, how they are created; then you can manage them. Ask the right questions.

For sure you can manipulate the consciousness; equally you can manipulate your ego. But ask yourself which one is more important to you. The paths are different; the end is the same.

You are restless today.

It is good that you get close to what you have created, close to nature, pure creation. You understand it; you feel it. You feel so good when you are with nature; you will. It is a pure form of creation. There are many forms of creation, many different types of energy.

You are not ready to live in the mental world; you would feel like you were isolated in a desert. You cannot comprehend this world. You must continue.

Ask yourself, how is it possible to travel at two-hundred kilometers in one hour on a high speed train, and sit down and read a book at the same time?

Note:
1. *Answer to my question asked mentally before meditation: for a matter of convenience, is there a name by which we could call you?*

Session 6 - 29/04/2022

Everything has a meaning. You are constantly creating. You must recognise what the meaning is for you. You must separate; you must analyse. Even the smallest things that you create have a meaning. The cause and effect. You can only go so far; you are still controlled by your conditioning. It is necessary. Your journey is infinite. Everybody wants to understand the meaning of their lives. Many are afraid to ask the question; they fear the answer. There is nothing to fear. It is a wondrous journey of discovery. You are building your own staircase so you can rise above, above and beyond.

Do not be afraid. You will only be affected by others. You allow them to affect you. You are afraid to decide. The message is always the same; you only keep asking the question because you are uncertain. You must know. I will repeat it in a different way, every time you ask, I will tell you in a different way. The question is always the same. What you do with the information is for you to decide.

If you help others, then you help yourself. That is universal. If you slow them down, then you slow down yourself. That is also universal. You cannot harm; this doesn't exist. Again, the message is the same. You always look at it as a point in time. It is not what you think. There is no time as you think. Every point in time is the same point, in the same way that all the data you need to access is within you. Carry it with you always, metaphysically or physically. Your questions lead to one point, always.

In your timeline here, things will change dramatically in the physical world; you know this. This will not change your direction. It has already altered your position, but it will never change your direction. Position, direction, it's different, leading to the same conclusion. I am here to help you understand, to rationalise. It is difficult for me also. You would say we are from different cultures, different worlds, when in reality we are the same.

Knowing will set you free. Do not be afraid of knowledge or wisdom. Many people are; it evokes change. You don't like change. You think you do, but you don't. You are conditioned not to like change. You are conditioned to retract against change. You think it is a natural feeling. It is not. It is a conditioned feeling. Many will not change. They refuse. This is not bad for them. It is what they chose, how they feel, how they have been affected by their emotions, their fears. It does not mean they are lost. Do not judge them; it is futile, performs no function.

You will be shown the things you ask, what you call science. You have been shown a lot. You will continue learning, experiencing. You are driven by your ego, of course. It is the driving force behind your questions, and you do know how to separate it, but not always. You will always revert back to your conditioning whilst you are here. For you it is a natural course. Don't try and fight this; you can't. Allow it; acknowledge it. I know you are tired, but it is necessary. Many will learn, more importantly, they will know. You must always know.

Ask yourself, where did that thought come from, why did I think that at that time in this world? Why did I think it? It is not an accident, although your mind will tell you it was. We both have incredible creative thoughts. This is the reason you are on this journey. There is no barriers for your thoughts, but they are at tangents, creating many chaotic situations. This is not wrong, but there is an easier way.

Your conditioning screams out to name everything, to give me a name. There is no necessity to do this. You have asked me on many occasion what my name is. I am not a name. I am an energy, an entity. I am you. I told you before, I am Seth. It is the same thing. You would not understand that, because you are screaming to give me a brand, an identity, a name. It is not important.

There are no boxes to put things in, to separate them, to isolate them. They don't exist. Everything is in one place. Your desire to put something in a box is your desire to control it, to own it, to imprison it. Freedom is not sitting in a box. This is the problem with your science. They are determined to put it in a box. If only they knew it doesn't belong in a box. It is a whole piece. It is all connected with everything in the metaphysical and everything in the world; it is all connected, your world that is.

Do you not know how small your box is? Do you not realise how tiny it is? It is so insignificant that it doesn't even exist. It is so small, this little box you create, this little box that you sit in. Correct energy that is necessary for you to experience, you cannot get through the box. It cannot get into the box. You are preventing it from getting into the box, your box, your one of many boxes.

A square is a block. A circle is eternal. It is infinite. Think about that. So many sides on a square, only one on a circle. The sphere, again, symbolic of the world you live in. Circles and squares, it is important that you look at the shapes. They have an effect. The symbols have an effect. The tiniest moment in your life, it has an effect. You will shrug it off as being insignificant. It has an effect. So much, so many particles, the jigsaw is infinite. You can harness a square object; you cannot harness a round object. It's significant, closer to answering your questions… I know.

You ask me what is your purpose. The question is insignificant. You do not even understand the question you ask. It does not fit in my world. It's difficult for me to answer. I would like to say, experience is merely all it is, but it is more. It is more that you wouldn't understand. It is more I cannot answer, not that you would understand it. Purposes, ego. Ego is a tool. Ego is not knowing. So therefore, it's impossible to answer the question "what is your purpose". It is insignificant. This is why it is so difficult to cross over, to explain, to understand. But you are where you should be; that's all I can tell you. Know it, know it inside, you are where you should be.

<h3 style="text-align:center"><u>Session 7 - 12/05/2022</u></h3>

Do not stray from the path you have chosen. Do not deviate from the path you have chosen. There is many things you don't understand, and there are many reasons why you are on this path. You have chosen a difficult path. All the answers lie within. Keep searching; keep looking; keep listening. You will know.

What is occurring now in your world is accelerating fast. It has little consequence to your future. It's difficult for you to separate; I know this. You are still trying to put everything in your box. This is not where you will find your answers. You do have a reason to be here, but it is not what you think it is. You have to find it. You have to know it. Your ego will always rationalise a reason for you to be here, but that is not the reason. Being frustrated is part of the process. Frustration is an emotion. Being inquisitive is part of the process. Inquisitive is your ego. Stay on the path. I will not advise you what your path is; it is. That is not why I am here. I will only confirm to you what you are already thinking.

You live in such a small world; you have such a tiny perspective of that world. Do you think it's a competition? It's not. You are always trying to position yourself within it at a point that is higher than the last one. There are indeed nine points, nine positions, but then the cycle starts again, back to number one, which is infinite.

Self-enlightenment is not a competition, neither is it a game. It is peace from within, knowing. It is simple; it is not complicated. You make it complicated. It is love from within. Project the emotion of love, and everybody will feel it. I know in here it sounds so simple, and it is, but out there I know it's different for you.

By understanding the origin of the source, you will understand self. There are many species out there that do not understand the origin of the source. They are like you. They understand the tools they have better than you, but they do not understand the source. They merely accept the source. They are intrigued about you and your journey. It is intense, but their intrigue is no concern of yours. It is your journey; it's not theirs.

Life does have a meaning. The creation of energy is a meaning. And the transmission of emotions creates energy, transmitted through frequencies. All has a meaning. You already understand the technicalities. There is no necessity to confuse yourself.

Even in your world there are some that are blessed with a higher knowing, even higher than what you call ET. That faith is often blind, which makes it pure. Recognise it. Know it.

You cannot tell others what to do. You cannot have an effect on their life. You can help them; you can guide them. Not all will respond, but many will. Do not deny your reason. Separate yourself from the confusion; isolate the confusion. It's only interference. Keep the channel open; keep it clean; keep it pure. Interference cannot harm you if you don't allow it to.

The information lies within; the ignition of that information lies outside; it's the outside that will bring it in.

Your senses are very heightened now. Stay on the journey.

Session 8 - 16/05/2022

Your time in this world is approaching fast. It is necessary for you to know. You have learned a lot in the times we have met. It is necessary for you to apply this knowledge. There is much more to learn, but you know enough. And it's also difficult for you to step outside of your box as it is everybody. But you know why; you understand why.

Many will be left behind. You don't have to worry about these people. It's not of your concern. Awareness is knowing. It is not a gift as you term a gift. You can only guide; you cannot interfere. Interference will change your own direction; guidance will force it in a positive way. Others must look within just like you look within, but it's their choice. If they choose not to, then that's their choice.

You are constantly looking within for an explanation of most things, and you will find it; you write it.

Energy is an incredibly powerful thing. You do not truly know how it works. The mind is an incredibly powerful tool.

You want to apportion blame for what is happening in your world. You are to blame too. The mind will always choose the easiest route; the consciousness will always choose the hardest route. So many people have chosen the easiest route. They are only the same as you, but they have made a different choice. If you want to apportion blame to them, there is no blame. They are the same as you. They are you. You want to single them out; they are the same. They don't even know what they are doing. Energy in their mind is too strong. They don't even recognise their consciousness. They don't understand it, no awareness of it. They are blinded with their minds. This is why it has no concern for you. You can't change it; you can't alter it. They create their own position; you must create yours.

What lies outside that you are so fascinated with is no difference to what lies inside, because it is the same. You choose whatever you want to do, or however you want to do it.

The reason you have no memories when you begin your journey is that your memories would just confuse you. You would not be able to complete your journey. The erasure of your memories is necessary for you to complete your journey, to remember. After all, your memories are conditioned. The only importance is your consciousness, not your memories. You have to ask yourself, what is self? What am I? Who am I? Where am I?

Separation from a materialistic world does not mean isolation from self. It does not mean isolation from others. They are the same thing. It's the same message again and again and again. It is a simple message; it is not complicated. It is not complicated in here. It is complicated out there for you to separate. I think you can deal with the interference now, because you understand it, interference being the interference of others, other situations, other lives. I think you have learnt how to separate the two. Now you need to apply that separation. You need to apply what you have learned.

You will be helping others, but you won't be aware that you are. It's a natural occurrence. It's a natural occurrence from the source. Even your closest will question you. In fact, probably more they will question you. You have to remain strong. Know inside that your experience is correct. They will question you through their own fears, through their own interpretation of what is real and what is not.

If you choose not to experience any longer the power of self, then that is fine. But I do not think this will happen. Do not entice into your life complications; there is no necessity for you to do this now. The path is very clear to you. You can deny it, but it is clear. It is a clear channel, a pure channel, a pure channel from the source. The only person that will not allow this journey is yourself through your fear, your conditioning.

I know your questions are relevant. I know you are only interested in the discovery of self. Practical matters I know you are not interested in; you see no necessity for this. One sits much higher than the other. Carry on with your journey, your experience. It may seem relentless sometimes, but it is not.

Use your imagination to apply what you have learnt, what you know. A wondrous journey.

Note:
I coughed throughout the session, but John never spoke at the same time. He systematically waited, unconsciously knowing when I was going to cough, as if not to pollute the recording.

Session 9 - 18/05/2022

As a species you have been controlled from the beginning of your time. The energy that controls you is metaphysical, and you were created for this purpose. It is also energy from the source. It is the same. It is for you to decipher what it is that you need to create. You will lift yourself out of this control. This is the purpose of the moment of the time you are in. The controlling energy is not wrong as you would term wrong. It is for you to know.

You create all the complexities that you see and hear. You entwine the energy within the creations. You give it value; you give it strength; you give it justice, when really it is only you. You give it numbers; you give it names. Your creation from the beginning of time, what you call time here, it is only energy. Your complicated way of naming everything confuses you. You confuse yourself. You feed it; you feed it with your fear. You live in such a small box. You pass your time away with such insignificant subjects. There is no necessity to do this; you already know. The only reason that this energy interferes with your life is because you allow it. You feed it; you support it. You must rise above it. You have created your own prison. You water it like you water a garden. You have all the tools to do the job, and yet you still make it so complicated. You have created a fantastic story, and you have fed it. And now you must destroy the story and move forward, move up so many levels. And once again, you are at the beginning, number one.

Yes, it is clear, very clear. Do you not find it strange that it is so clear in here, and yet out there it is not? Do you not ask yourself why? You choose to be wherever you are, whenever you are, whatever point in time you want to be. Time is an illusion, your illusion.

I must keep repeating to you: there is no good; there is no bad. They are the same thing, only energy. It's very difficult for you to understand this… I know. It's important now that the energy is balanced. Do not fear. You cannot even comprehend the beauty that lies outside of self, neither the beauty that lies within. Creations that you can create, the source, everything is correct.

Throw away your crutches that you have created, for an illness you don't have, and see how fast you can run.

<u>Session 10 - 21/05/2022</u>

You have both played this game many times before, together, always opposing factors, one positive, one negative, one plus, one minus. The setting is irrelevant. The meaning is the same. Centuries in what you call time, the roles have changed many times. The ego-created roles have changed within you on many occasions. One is a crutch for the other, an opposite, an opposite energy, but the destination is the same. This time it's no longer a game: this is a conclusion.

I don't have to explain to you the principles anymore. It is knowing this that will allow you to continue your journey. I have told you it doesn't matter what is occurring at the moment; it is of no relevance. It is an individual journey. You help each other, but there is only a limit to what you can do. You have to go from within.

You are being watched, but it is of no concern to you. You are being watched through intrigue. They are intrigued as you are intrigued. They understand the technology, and they are able to utilise it to watch you, but it has no significance. They too are learning like you are. They know better than to intervene, they know it is not correct; that's why they don't. This is why they do not intervene: it will have a negative impact on them.

There is little more I can tell you that you don't already know. So you must practice; you must experiment; you must use your imagination to create. It is time for action. I cannot really explain the metaphysical to you, you cannot comprehend it. You will apply your logic from here to there; it does not work. You will automatically do this; I am sure you feel it.

I will not leave; I will not leave you. I am you. How could I leave?

There is no point to confuse you. You can create so many symbols, numbers, colours, so many sounds. Whilst on this journey this will confuse you. Symbolism is very important, and I'm sure you see it many times. But also it will confuse you. So much information, the information highway, but again, it will confuse. You do recognise the symbols often, but they are confusing to you, not knowing how you place them within your thought process. For you a cross is symbolic.

Yes, you can see so many pictures; I know. So many colours, all created by your imagination, but very symbolic.

Every path is written, every path, and so many to choose from. You choose.

<u>Session 11 - 23/05/2022</u>

Clear and precise is as it should be. What is above is below; it is the same thing. It must be clear to you; it must be obvious. You will know. Information is confusing. Radio waves can be confusing, nondescript, but you will know. You do know. There are many trying to do what you are doing now. The door has opened, but you have a clear channel. It is by no accident. I am not the source; I am like you. I have a higher understanding than you do, but it is the same.

Many are seeking now to understand the source. A race in time in what you would call time, but it's not a race; it's not a game. Competition is invalid; it has no meaning. You are close. You are driven by your intrigue as are we all, but your intrigue often confuses you as does it all. Keep it simple, because it is.

There are so many forms of energy, of what you call ET, so many forms, metaphysical and physical forms, so many. Do you want to literalise that one form would take over your world? It's irrelevant. Your world is tiny. An endless journey for you, an endless journey for everyone.

The subconscious mind of the human has created many forms, often confusing, deliberately confusing. Many symbols, many forms, all with the same purpose, created through fear. Names, brands, organisations, all irrelevant. Same thing. You have to step outside of this. You have to look from outside within. You do. They will control many with this. They are. But again, for your journey it's irrelevant. But I think you know this. Your purpose is to understand this, to know it. How could it be that simple? It is that simple.

You always want to help. You always want to intervene. Your compassion, your ego, it's on fire. By helping yourself you will help others; it is a natural course. By intervening, likely you will hinder others; this is also a natural course. Your conditioned life taught you this.

The source is love; it knows no different. Your world talks about love as though it knows. It has not a clue. In the name of love, you chant it like a bedside story. It truly does not know what love is, the energy, the frequency, the power.

There are many obstacles for you, but you can overcome them. You create a problem to solve it. You might not think you do, but that is exactly what you do, like a pastime. There is no need to create it in the first place, but you do, constantly. And when you solve it, you feel good. The whole process is futile, and you do it over and over again. You do it consciously, and you do it subconsciously. Create a problem, solve a problem, feel good. Create a problem, don't solve a problem, feel bad. Over and over again. What would you do in a world without problems? Ask yourself: what would you think about? What would you create? Ask yourself: if there was no problems in my world, what do I do today? Your interpretation of what you do would be based on your conditioning. Try to step away from that, and ask the same question.

Pacification is knowing *(1)*. This is real. You ask that question many times. It is real. Many times I tell you it is not for me to tell you what to do. In the process I can explain, the choice is yours *(2)*. You can be compassionate to others, but at the same time you can block their intent, their effect on you. You can block this, but it doesn't mean you are not compassionate. They are you. They are also frightened like you are *(3)*.

The dividing factors in your world will create an opportunity for many, but more it will not. You recognise this. A coming together is one, number one, one energy, one source. A separation is also one, but not recognised by the individual. So therefore, it feels like many, but it is still only one. Self-realisation of this will guide you. It will lift you; it will raise you. Yes, it all seems so simple in here *(4)*, and out there it is a jungle… I know.

You can create anything you want to create. Some people choose to create demons—that's your words, demons. They only exist in the form that they exist within themselves. There is nothing for you to fear. This is child, child creation. Again, chosen, chosen by the individual to entwine, to engage, to participate. You have a desire to always participate, to brand, to name, to belong. If only you knew you have always belonged to the source. You are a part of the source, and yet you crave to separate yourself, always.

Your practicality often slows you down. Your desire to tick all the boxes, in your words *(5)*. Your fear of pain slows you down. It's not pain; it's an illusion. The very thing you don't want to create you do create. Now that's irony through fear. You wish it upon yourself, but you don't think you do.

You have to simplify your thought process. Whilst it's complex on one hand, it really is not. You have to overview. Same questions, different analysis. Repetitive, simple, but for you, complicated. Engage, disengage, engage, disengage, you love it. Experience, it's a beautiful thing, and you don't even recognise that.

Visualisation is most important. Visualisation from imagination is key, key to create, create the wave, create the motion, the energy formation.

Notes:
1. *Pacification: A term I often use, a means for some aliens to be accepted and to annihilate any human opposition (Warning of the New Message). I have often wondered if John's channeling was an attempt at manipulation, especially since he saw and felt a 'Little Grey' in the cave... The answer is clear: when we Know, we understand that fighting makes no sense.*
2. *It could also be the entities, including the 'Grey', seen and felt by John in the cave. It is up to us to give them importance or not.*
3. *Similarly, probably in reference to this 'Grey' that seemed lost, and even if it is a species that controls, they deserve our compassion, being a part of ourselves.*
4. *In the cave.*
5. *I take this directly for myself: solar panels so in my head I'm afraid of running out of energy, reserves of food and drinking water, a vegetable garden, a house far from floods possible, difficult to access so as not to be bothered. In fact, I have ticked all the boxes given in the New Message to prepare for a difficult period...*

<u>Session 12 - 27/05/2022</u>

You must try to feel divine love, not what you call love; it is a tiny morsel of the true feeling of divine love. Divine love encompasses everything and everyone. No one is left behind. It is difficult for you to do this. The love you feel for your children, for your family, your friends, it is exaggerated by so much of divine love. This is what you are swimming back to. This is where you are going. We know this, and we understand it. You have it within. You are searching for it, and you are not aware that is what you are searching for.

We are given many names, many brands, and they are the same. You have to analyse everything. Sometimes, what you think is correct is not necessarily correct. Motives, reasons, many have ulterior motives and reasons created by themselves within their world. Their world is not the world; it is only their world. Of course, more confusion. The confusion is unnecessary, created by yourself.

The source is all of the emotional energy together as one. Separation is by your choice. As one or together, it is your choice, the same thing.

If you want to work with us on a practical basis, then it's possible. But there's no necessity for this. You merely have to understand. Practicality is the same thing. Your conditioned mind would create us as ET—is what you would call us—but it is only your conditioning that would do this. There is no differential between any of us. Your words make it very confusing for us also, your interpretation, your application, confusing. It is one. We are the same.

Practicality applied in our world is much different than practicality applied in your small world. You have to look from outside within to understand this. I know you are confused about practicality and application. Knowing is application; knowing is practicality; one follows the other. It is not so complicated. Everything works on frequencies, the energy from the source.

You are moving in the correct direction. This channel is clear; it is pure; it is without interference. It is necessary for you to understand. I said many times in here, it is much different to out there. Fulfillness is knowing. Know thyself. You are fixated on so many pastimes, so many creations, but the truth is simple. You are raising the frequencies and the vibrations. You are doing it now. We do not fully understand the source ourselves, but we too are travelling in that direction, like you. It helps us to help you. This we do know.

I do not talk to you individually. You are one.

If you create a carnival in your life, then you will live in a carnival. It is what you create. We only choose to focus on what is real, not something from your imagination, or creation that we know is not real. That is why we don't like names and brands. You relate to this. You warm to it. You create a story around it. But it is not real. I won't even say the names that you create for us because it's a diversion. It is wasted energy. That's why I won't say it. It is confusing for you. You create your own confusion. It is best to be simple, to know the source. I can play with your words if you want me to, but it's **unnecessary**.

I have been with you for a very long time in what you call time. With us you built many things on this world, many.

Positive and the negative needs to be balanced once again.

Every time you meditate you will be filled with light; you will be filled with love. As your day progresses it will soon disappear, but you will be drawn back again.

It is pure; it is pure light. This we can show you *(1)*.

We will speak to you more now in the day. You will know, you will know which direction to go. You have come a long way, but there is a long way to go.

Note:
1. John's vision in real time.

<u>Session 13 - 31/05/2022</u>

You are constantly in one emotional state or another, constantly and consciously. When you speak with words, it is not the words that are important. It is transmission of the emotional state combined with the words that are important. It is the intent behind the words that are important, the intention. You have created words for your form of communication. They can be misleading due to the emotional intention behind the word. It is important for you to understand this, to feel it.

In our world there is only emotion. This is how we communicate, through frequencies. This is also why you get very confused. Your mind will analyse the words, but your mind will not understand the emotion behind those words. Often, when you are communicating with someone you will feel a different emotion. Likely, this is their emotion, not yours. You must learn how to separate two channels. One is correct; often one is not correct.

It is far more important to understand your own emotions; understand how you create them, why you create them, how you transmit them, how you react to them, why you react to them. Based on understanding your own emotions, you will know then how to react to other people's emotions. Words are a very primitive form of communication.

Action is not described in a physical form. Action is described in a mental form, a metaphysical way from within *(1)*. Action will bring reaction. We are all one. Change the thoughts, you create an action. When it is applied, it will create a reaction, pure energy. Although you understand all of this, you are still stuck in your conditioned world. It is not easy for you to apply. You are drawn back constantly to your conditioning. This is correct. It is pointless to be frustrated, even though frustration is an energy.

Just continue. It will reveal itself to you. Then life will change; it will become very different. People will know you have changed. They won't really understand why, but they will feel it. They will want to be a part of it. They won't know why, but they will. It is universal love. It is the divine source of love, an energy, an unstoppable force. This is action: knowing thyself. You are a part of everyone, and everyone is a part of you. You cannot avoid this. You can detain it, but it is inevitable. It will be released. The vibration needs to be raised. It is the same for everyone.

You are birthing and rebirthing all the time, constantly. The cycle of energy continues. We too are the same, birth, rebirth. You will ask why? I cannot explain this to you. It is like the constant production of energy, the creation of imagination, birth, rebirth, birth, rebirth. There is no escape from this. This is what you are, a pure form of energy.

You cannot comprehend the size of an infinite universe. It's impossible for you. You cannot comprehend the volume of structures within it, the mass. It is incredible. Neither can we, but it is upon an infinite one.

Yes, you can see my eye. I will appear to you *(2)*.

We have learned the physics of the universe, the world ……. *(Transcript from audio impossible)* physically or metaphysically, because we understand the physics. You do not yet understand the physics. You are learning.

We do not interfere. It is to our determent if we interfere. We guide; we confirm; we challenge. Challenge is not interfering. We do not impose; we respect.

Our form is not your form. All metaphysical forms have a structure. It is a little bit like a DNA structure. All physical forms have a DNA structure. All metaphysical forms have a DNA structure or similar. All frequencies carry a specific structure, their interpretation designated by value, value for their effect. This is created from the source. It is energy, pure. Value for purpose, value for creation, for direction, we have created many forms using this energy. The technology would be beyond your understanding. The ability to appear and disappear would be beyond your understanding. The ability to be able to travel in time within a second would be beyond your understanding.

I know you are inquisitive; it is natural. Stay on the journey. You will truly see what you can do, what you can create.

Notes:
1. *Probably due to a lack of action, we wonder what type of action we should take on our journey. In fact, no physical action is really required on our part, only better understanding and clearer thoughts.*
2. *At this moment, John was having a vison of a huge black almond eye.*

Session 14 - 03/06/2022

If you are aware of emotions, you can change an emotional feeling into a physical feeling at will. You can choose to feel it physically. This is the origin of illness. Because of your erratic emotions, you are constantly changing these emotions into a physical feeling without awareness, without knowing.

I know you sensed my presence on entering the cave. I am not here to harm you *(1)*. We choose to be a form or not a form. We are all the same, all connected. What I show you is what I know. How could I show you something I don't know? It's impossible. There are many forms; some communicate; some don't. It is their choice. And it is your choice to discern between those forms, what you believe is, or what you know, not believe, what you know is correct.

The higher self is making its way back to the source. We too. There is nothing to fear from us. I have said to you before, when we are helping you, we are helping ourselves. This is the reason we help. For you it would appear selfish, but it's not. Because we are all connected, there is no selfish. It is from the source. Isolated and wanted to be connected: this is awareness.

So, we choose to be a physical form, or we do not. I know you desire to meet us in a physical form. This is possible. You have to be prepared for this. You think you are, but in reality you are not. We will come.

It is very difficult for you to rationalise. You apply always your conditioned world, your conditioning. It is determined by how much emphasis you put on conditioning in a physical world and the metaphysical world, the mental world. Everything is determined by your perception of this, by your reliance of it. Cross contamination, that's what it is.

People are awakening all over your world. It is not only us that are talking to these people; there are many. There are many levels of this awareness and understanding. Your communication channels are open, and people are talking about contact. It is only you that know that it is correct or not correct. It is only you that can discern. There will be lots of confusion. It all boils down to one thing, that is emotion, your feeling. How do you feel when you listen? It is very simple, but also very confusing for you. You must ask yourself, how do I feel? What do I feel? I think you know why you feel.

You must remember everything is possible in a mental world; so therefore, your physical form is irrelevant. Your physical needs, your physical desires, irrelevant. The possibilities are endless, infinite. One completely outweighs the other, a step up the ladder. It took us a long time in what you call time to recognise this ourselves, to recognise it within other species, to understand it, to understand the separation between the conscious and the consciousness. Through technology we can separate, but it is not your technology. It is the technology of the source through frequencies. Through emotions we can separate body, physical to mental. And we can choose to live in both if we wish. And we do. But for you this is an astronomical experience. For you it is huge. But there is no need to fear it. Remember, we can choose the form we wish to appear to you. We can choose whatever form we like. We will always try to choose a form that will not shock you or surprise you, or we can change the form. But the emotion doesn't change. The feeling, that will always be a constant. We cannot change this. We can utilise it always, but we cannot change it. It is the source.

You know these things, and you are communicating with the source, not with us, with the source. We are utilising that position. We are capitalising on that position. We too are communicating with the source, almost like a translator in the middle. This is why you are protected. Your protection doesn't come from us; it comes from the source. We, like you, are observers. We are learning like you are. Although we are more advanced than human technology, the source's technology, we are still learning; we are still communicating.

Stop trying to rush it in your time. It is happening. And within your time it will happen *(2)*. Within its own time it already happened. You must also enjoy peace in here, the tranquility, the love, soon forgotten out there, soon confused out there.

You must show compassion to all species, both human and both what you would call ET. Your imagination would determine one as being bad, and one as being good. There is no bad, and there is no good. They are all of the origin of the source. Confused maybe, good, no, bad, no. This is judgment. I told you before, judgment does not exist in our world. It is a fallacy. But your conditioned life will always judge, good, bad, kill, destroy. There is only love.

Control. You are always playing these games in your world. Your conditioning is necessary for you to advance and raise your frequency. But realisation of this must let go of your conditioning. You call it detachment. It is not detachment. You are not detaching; you are joining. You are joining the source, the way back. We too are on the same journey, the way back. We are not detaching; we are joining—your words again, it is so difficult —but it is sometimes necessary to detach to learn. But you are not detaching *(3)*.

I know sometimes you don't like the change in yourself. You feel it, the fear of letting go of your conditioning. Do not be frightened. There is no necessity to be frightened. There is nothing to fear. It is only an advancement of yourself. Do not judge your conditioning. There is a reason that it exists. You chose it for that reason. You chose it. Your path is clear, maybe not to you, but it is very clear. You are here, that is clear. Ask yourself why? Ask yourself why you are here? That is very clear. Enjoy it, enjoy the moment, the peace, the love.

Remember, from all the emotions of all the people in your world, cross contamination will be very prevalent on the internet. Imagine the emotions, imagine the mass of emotion that is transcribed and you receive. You must know if something is real or it is not. You must know. You do know.

One source, one universe, one people: this is truth.

Notes:
1. *We are still suspicious of him.*
2. *I often talk about interaction with aliens, sometimes with a certain impatience. Is that what this is about? Maybe, because he refers to them a few lines later...*
3. *I often speak about this notion of detachment, in reference to the teachings of the New Message, and with my Buddhist buddy Gilou.*

Session 15 - 04/06/2022

Although your journey seems chaotic, it is not. There is a uniform, a pattern that exists. It is necessary for you to understand this. You chose this journey. You might ask why? There are many reasons. You have experienced it many times before, a different story, the same journey. It is necessary to understand the uniform, the pattern.

Memories of your dependency in your different lives are unimportant. To understand the source is all that is important. It is true that you are trapped in cycles of life, but only through choice, not trapped. You choose to experience the same things over and over again. You are becoming aware of this. We no longer have to complete these cycles. We understand fully what it means, but we do not fully understand the source. You are coming to the end of the cycles to begin a different journey. You need to be prepared for this journey. You are now preparing for this journey. We will help you. We are helping you. The answer will always be love, not your love, but love from the source, love and light.

Your world seems a crazy place at the moment. It is not. It is necessary. You are the lucky ones, but you have earned it. You have suffered much pain, much anguish, many emotions. It is time now you understood why. Do not consider times, dates, hours. We do not really understand this. Our emotional feeling is now, but what is occurring now is going to occur now. Change is imminent, in the moment. Again it's difficult for you to understand this. It has a uniform pattern. Your world has overlayed different dimensions. This is what is occurring. This is why it is in what you would call turmoil, but necessary. There seems to be no sense to it as far as you're concerned, but there is. Look on it as a challenge. Your world is being challenged. It's not forced. There are many trying to manipulate, but they have no idea of what is occurring. They are merely trying to take advantage of a situation, driven by their conditioning. They have no real clue what is going on; opportunists is what they are, no understanding of the source. A great change, you have seen it all before, opportunism, dictatorship, control, death and life.

Your growth is exponential, separated or one; you choose.

We do not have illness where we are from. We do not grow old. We do not kill each other. We do not kill others. We create what we wish. We live where we wish. There is no reason for us to eat or drink, but we do because we take pleasure from this. If we need minerals, we create them. We use our energy to form them through frequencies. We can create any type of particle through frequencies. If we wish to live in a physical world, we create it. We all know how to do this. We all know what is correct. We all know how it works, how it is applied. There is no necessity to oppose each other, to destroy each other. I laugh when I see you doing this on the planet you live. It's due to confusion.

Male and female is the same for us. We can choose to be one or the other if we wish to. We can choose to integrate if we wish to, as either or both. One of your longstanding separations is between male and female, when in fact they are the same. Your conditioning did this, created opposition, challenged, created competition, when in reality you are the same thing as we are.

When you have what you call an out of body experience—we live that way permanently—you have the desire to return quickly. You fear being out of body for long periods of what you call time. Your urge to go back is very strong, to go back to your conditioned life. You can travel in space and time to any position when you have an out of body experience, but your conditioning stops you doing this.

We can travel in a physical form, and we can travel in a mental form, and we can travel anywhere we like in an instant. But travelling is ok, but you need to know where you are going. You need to know why you are travelling, for what purpose. We do not just stick a pin in a map of the universe and go. It is a very deep environment. We do not know the full scope of this environment. We cannot map it. We do not know, and we do not engage until we know.

This is the key, knowing. This is what we are trying to show you. Know. Do not think you know. Know. Knowing means there is no discrepancy; there is no question; there is no wrong, no right; it is final; it is complete. When you know, you have no more fear, no more questions to ask. It is relatively simple if you think about it in those terms. It only becomes a problem for you when you don't know.

Session 16 - 09/06/2022

You must be precise. You must be accurate. You must adapt with what you have been taught. There are many things you can change now. The energy is vast. Your world has waited a long time in what you call time for this moment. Many are trying to adapt; many are trying to change. You have an advantage; you know the rules of the game. But it is not a game.

Your fear is diminishing; this is good. You are at one with yourself now. Now you can move forward. We are watching and monitoring your progress. It is good. You have already noticed people's reception of you; it is changing. It is lifting. It is positive. It is the source. Of course, it is clear in here, and of course it is confusing out there. It is for you to discern the difference, and always apply it. What I have told you is correct, this is how it works. There is no need to question the theory anymore. It is not theory. It is the truth.

We can communicate much easier within this cave than we can out there. There is so much interference for you both out there. There are many what you would term lost souls out there at this moment in your time. This is correct. Forever lost can be an instant found within a second, and forever is a second. So you don't have to worry about them or be concerned. Their journey is the same as yours. They are one; they are you; you are them; we are you. It is the same.

You can shift the energy. There are many people doing this now. You can shift it; you can change it. You can alter the timeline that you are in. There has been a shift in a more positive or plus direction recently. The energy has changed. The formation of the particles have changed. This is an accumulation of everybody's emotions. Many more people are becoming aware. The fire is dwindling. You can feel it yourself. The positive charge, the positive direction, the positive lift, you can feel it within yourselves, both of you. Your own life, the negative will attack you again. I am not talking about an individual attack; I am talking about a very powerful energy. But I think you can deal with it now. You understand it more. You understand it is the same as you.

The journey is good. You may not think so, but the journey is good; the experience is good. If you do not experience, you will never know. If you do not search, you will never know. If you do not look, you surely will never know. This is why sometimes for you it feels like a rollercoaster, an up and down motion. It is, it is necessary for you. Too many ups and you will lose yourself within it. Too many downs and it is difficult for you to get up. There is a balance that lies in the middle. This is what you are trying to achieve, a knowing. I say again: know thyself; know yourself inside and you will know. Both are necessary, minus and positive, minus and plus, positive and negative, all necessary. There are moments in time where every single soul understands this, but their illusion of time will soon lose the moment, and the moment is lost until it is found again. And it is always found again. You need to find it, and you need to keep it.

Don't worry about your future. You define it; you create it; you are creating it. Remember, all the knowledge you need, you already have inside. You just need to remember. Wisdom is something else. Remembered knowledge acquires wisdom. Wisdom is never lost; wisdom is knowing. It is not knowledge. In your world knowledge is power. Power is unnecessary from knowledge, only wisdom. Wisdom is the real power, the power of love, the power from the source. You do not need to set out on a journey to acquire knowledge. You already have it within, within your brain, within your mind. You merely need to awaken it, to tap into it, into that source. That is not the source. Although it is from the same place, it is not the source.

I know your fear is being removed. I know you can feel differently. It is necessary. It is good. It is energy from the source. You cannot be harmed by the people that have not yet awoken. It is impossible. No matter how devious you think they are, they cannot harm you. They are not aware of what they are doing. You must forgive them; you must send them the love from the source, the energy. It is not wrong what they do; there is no wrong. They are mistaken, merely mistaken; on their journey they are mistaken. This is how you lift the frequency. This is how you lift the energy, the power, in a positive direction. The love from the source, all powerful, all seeing, all knowing, in your words God—it is the source.

Religions are like words; they can be manipulated, manipulated by the minds of men and women. The message is important, not the religion. The emotion, the frequency that carries the message is only important, the wakening from that frequency, that emotion. It doesn't matter about the story. The story is unimportant, just like your conditioned life, unimportant. It is the message that is carried through the emotion that is received by the person; it is the only thing that is important. This is the source. Intent, intentional, do it with intent. Mean it. Know it.

Session 17 - 12/06/2022

You must understand that you have to experience the world you have chosen to live in. You have to participate. You have reached a certain point of understanding, but this is not necessarily the complete and end point. Therefore, you must participate. But realisation of this will make you think you do not have to participate. But you chose, you chose the vehicle you are in. You chose to feel all of those emotions. You have to be a part of that. Sometimes, you won't feel like participating based on your knowledge, your wisdom, but you must participate.

Many around you will be intrigued by the changes you make within yourself. You will reflect that. They will feel it. It is difficult for them to understand. In the moment they can understand. When the moment is gone, they do not understand. The moment is all moments, but not in your illusion in your world, your world of time.

Your world is changing very quickly now. You could say behind the scenes there is a lot happening; a lot of changes are occurring. A lot of energy is shifting. You will see this soon. You do not need to be afraid. There are opposing forces also. I cannot tell you what the outcome will be, but it is necessary that the action takes place. You feel this. You know it. Do not be shocked by what you see happening. Do not fear it. There is nothing to fear. Many people will see it differently than you do. They will believe everything they are being told. It is no concern of yours.

I know it is difficult for you to live in both camps. It is difficult for you to often understand the metaphysical world, particularly when you are invested heavily in the physical world you live in. But again, this is necessary. It is a process. It is necessary for you to feel the process, to understand the love of the source. This is real love, real creation. We don't know any different than this. We know.

You can see the source in your world in everything that is created. You merely need to look, to examine, to examine all of people's emotions, examine all of the creations of this world. Every living thing has the source within it. You need to look, and you can see it. There is no necessity for us to prove this to you. You can see it every day of the week. You can see it; the source is in everything.

Why must you make your lives so complicated? Each one of you with so many emotions, emotions that you do not even know that exist, an infinite amount of a combination of emotions producing energy through frequencies. There are so many you cannot see. This makes your world very complicated for you, but you chose. You chose this complication. Through this complication you will be educated. And you will experience many different types of emotions, and you will learn how to adapt with these emotions, how to control them so you can move forward with your journey. Your future is very clear. It's very clear to us. I know it's not so clear to you, but it is very clear. Your now moment is very clear. You would determine future in time; it's not correct.

There are many messages coming through now from the metaphysical world to your world. More advanced, more advanced elements are sending through many messages to lift the vibration, coming from what you would call species, many species. But it doesn't matter what words you use to describe the elements. They're all one. They're all the same as you, from the source. There are many people transmitting this information to other people to try and lift them, to try and lift them onto the journey. It is having success. This is your journey, both of you. It is your journey. It is nobody else's journey. You chose it. You can leave at any time, but I know you won't. Your faith is strong.

Nobody will be left behind. There is no necessity for you to have concern about others. You only need to love them with the love from the source. That is all. And every, every living thing, it is you; it is I; it is all connected to the source. I tell you this over and over again, but it is necessary for you to hear it again. Your mind as soon as you leave this position deteriorates. Why it is necessary for me to keep repeating the same thing, is why you come in here, to listen, to experience. The channel in here is very clear; it is very precise. It is necessary.

Your steps are a step too far for most people. They will not understand. Nevertheless, you will talk to them. You will try to send them love, but it will be difficult for them to make this journey. They did not choose it. You know where you are going. You are remembering where you are supposed to go. Stay on the journey.

Session 18 - 15/06/2022

You have had many teachers in your lives. You have been inspired by many people. They are us; they are the same from the source. You will continue to be inspired by many people, many elements. It is your support, your support mechanism. It is necessary. We have been with you for a very long time in what you call time, yes time, your illusion, your made emotion. You are understanding more every day. You have known for a very long time in what you call time. Your understanding is getting greater.

There is nothing to fear. Removal of fear is freedom, free will. It is all happening for a very precise reason. The peace you feel in here is the peace you will feel everywhere. It is the same, from the source. You are understanding now more the complexity of the ego, the mind. You are understanding the manipulation. You still have work to do.

You will influence others. You may not be aware of this, but you will. It is not necessary that you are aware of this. It is unimportant; it is only your ego. It has always only ever been one. You are not isolated or separated, although you chose this route. It is only one.

We too are looking for more answers. We understand the philosophy better than you do so therefore, our questions are more precise than your questions. Your questions are based on your conditioning. Our questions are based on knowing, but we too are looking for answers, like you. Your development is intense. Every day you learn something different, something new, something you can apply. You learn how to let those thoughts pass through, the ones you think that you don't want to think. You are learning. I tell you again, your imagination is your most powerful tool, imagination through frequency, a creator of all physical, all particles.

The past, the present and the future are all one, in one moment. And you can change that moment. Nothing is defined; nothing is set in stone—your words. You are an amazing form of energy. Historically you created so many different circumstances for you to experience. Your understanding of this is what will set you free.

Do not pay so much attention to the mystics. They are stuck; they are fast; they are limited. They limit themselves. You have no limits. There is nothing you cannot do or create. I have told you before, you limit yourself with names and brands and circumstances you create yourself. They limit you. You limit yourself. You create your own pain. You may do it many times.

It is much simpler than you think it is, but then it always will be simpler in here. You know when something is correct inside. It kicks you. Listen to that. It is necessary for you to understand, like a kick in your stomach. You know. Do not ignore it. Do not make an excuse that it is not correct; it is correct. The symbols you see are only relevant because you created them within your world. They are relevant to you, your creation.

Man will follow, man will follow man always. Man would rather not use his imagination; he would rather use the imagination of another man. He will follow the imagination of another person. You must not do this. You must use your own imagination. It is very important for you to follow yourself. The process is very important. You can create amazing things with your imagination. Man follows man through fear. Yes, it is very clear.

It is very easy to latch onto a brand, to want it, to need it. It is easy to latch onto a name, a word. It is easier than the journey you are on. You will imprison yourself by doing this. And then you will have to wait in what you call time; you will have to wait until you know your realisation to release you. This is why you have created marketing. You market the mind, and the mind prevents the movement of the soul, the consciousness. A process that you repeat over and over again. You do this to create the energy of money. It has no relevance in our world. It has no form, no function; it is worthless. Part of your complex world, finance.

There is a universal code. I have told you before, although you think it is chaos, it is not. It is defined. It is defined through the production and the creation of matter. It is defined for a specific reason. It is a tool that you use when you create through your imagination. A uniform pattern exists. It appears random. It is sometimes random from your imagination. Your random thoughts are not necessary. It is the outcome that is important, the destination, the completion of the cycle, the journey to the source.

It is an advantage for me also to give you this information, to help you to understand. Subconsciously you have always received the information. To be consciously aware of it is an awakening for you, a call, a calling. How you react is your choice. How you apply is your choice. What we give you, we know, we do not think.

There are always two, but they are only one. Difficult for you, I know, to understand that. There are always two, but there is only one. They are the same. In your world there are billions, but there is only one. They are you. You can keep counting for an infinite time in what you call time, but there is only one.

You are always asking for proof. How much proof do you need? Every day you see proof; it is all around you. What you eat, what you see, when you sleep, it is full of proof, proof of the source. You can feel it in here. Through us you can feel the source. We are your channel. You are our channel. It is the same. You can't imagine the beauty that lies within. You can't imagine the creation that you can create, apply. You will.

Your futures are well aspected; they are well defined. Rise above, above and beyond. It is infinite, a cycle, a circle, a sphere. You can relax in knowing. You can relax in knowing, and you do know. You have always known. It is only an awakening for you, an awakening of your soul, your consciousness. And yes, it is very clear. I know you enjoy the peace and tranquility that exists within here. Meditation is a pure form of contact with the source.

Remember, your journey is endless. It is infinite. Infinity is only the moment. No beginning, no end, this is infinity. It is endless. It has no beginning; it has no end. Difficult for you to understand… I know. In a moment it can be changed; it can be altered; it can be recreated.

Peace, tranquility, love from the source is the pure energy that will keep you going, will drive you—it is driving you.

Session 19 - 18/06/2022

Everything in your world is an illusion created by you. You are a pure form of energy connected to the source. Your mind will try to keep you disconnected from the source; your consciousness will be attracted to the source. There is a defined reason for this. It is necessary. You will determine your energy as small or tiny. It is not. It is one. Your conditioning would call it small. This is your logic.

There is only one moment. There is no time as you determine time. It is one moment for every creation, every universe of which it is infinite. It is an infinite moment of one. This is difficult for you to understand. You cannot apply your logic to understand this. You will not be able to understand it. You have to raise your vibration to understand it.

Everything is connected to the source. You are not a physical being. You are a metaphysical being. You are a being of thought, a being of emotion, a being of frequency. You are energy. We are the same. We are you, and you are us, all connected, all one. When you know this, your world will be totally different.

It is your mind, your ego that confuses you. It is the love from the source that keeps you going. Yes, it becomes clearer in here; I know it does for you. It is comforting for you to hear these things, because when you leave the cave it is quickly forgotten… I know. But every time you hear these things your consciousness becomes more aware. It does not leave you, ever. It merely awakens more. It is necessary.

It is no good for me to explain to you what it is we are trying to learn from the source. You would not understand. But we are also intrigued like you are. We also wish to know more like you do. We are also on a journey like you are. When we help you, we are helping ourselves, because you are us. It is the same thing.

Being able to separate the ego from the consciousness or the soul as you call it, is the key. Of course, more difficult in practice. And as long as you are still breathing in the world you have created, it will never fully occur. It is an impossibility, for the very reason you are here. There is only a point you can reach. You are close. This is why you must not get frustrated. There is much more you can do to know yourself. It is an exciting journey. It is the reason you are here. And of course, when you are helping yourself, you will help others; it is a natural occurrence. People will be thrown into your life that you never knew before. They will be attracted to the energy. They will want to know. You are not responsible for these people. You don't owe them anything. There is no debt; it doesn't exist. There is only love.

The reason I talk to you like I do is because I know you don't want to know the detail. You don't ask for the detail. This is good. It's simple. If you need detail, then you don't know. The detail is unimportant. When I say detail, I am talking about your conditioned life and your conditioned lives. I am talking about all the crazy things that have been created through the energy, through the source, the crazy things in the universe. It is not necessary to see the physical element, or even know what it is. I know you know that. This is why the channel is pure, why it is clear. It is a lot to ask for some people. It is about faith. I told you before: faith can move mountains; it can also create them.

You are two opposites of energy which makes a perfect solution, but you are the same as we all are. I have no other description for you other than you are energy, because that's what you are. Your energy has created so many things in so much time, in what you call time. Your mind is taking a back seat now. Your consciousness is surfacing. This is good. This is the reason your ego is diminishing. This is through your choice; you chose it. You have created so many experiences.

You ask me how many others are experiencing this. It's irrelevant. There is only one. It is one. It is the same. Seven billion or one, it is the same number from the source. Again, you are trying to apply your logic, your conditioned logic. It does not work in the metaphysical world. It is like two different languages of spoken words, trying to communicate in two different languages, when neither understands the other. It's impossible. Yes, you are close to one. You have awakened many parts. You must continue. Always remember that there is a very good reason that you are here on this physical world that you created. It is not by chance. Be assured it is necessary and correct.

You are from different origins of creation, not necessarily the human species, but it is all the same. It is one, it is the same thing. Again, we are separating, you are separating. You are trying to define something. All I can tell you is that you are not all the same—it is all you need to hear—not all the same in the form you have chosen, and where that form's origin lay. But it's still the source. It is the same thing.

You will never deny what you are again. You have come to a junction, a point. You must stay on this journey. You will fill your life like you cannot believe is possible.

Session 20 - 20/06/2022

You will always find it difficult to establish purpose. Metaphysical purpose is much different than physical or conditioned purpose. Conditioned purpose implies ego, to win, to succeed, competition. Metaphysical purpose is much different than this. Metaphysical purpose is to feel, to feel the love from the source. Metaphysical purpose is one, the moment, infinity. So, when we use the word purpose, it is impossible to compare the two, because they are two different meanings completely. You struggle with this… I know. You cannot apply your physical world to purpose in the metaphysical world. It is impossible.

The moment is only now. It can be changed. It can alter. The energy can change. Your energy can change. The now moment are all moments in what you call time, historically and future. This again is hard for you to understand, but you will understand it. This is where you are going to. This is what you are leading to. Theoretically you can understand it, but you do not know. You cannot know in a physical realm. When you ask questions like how long have you been here, the answer that we would give is we never left. It is infinite. We are in the now as are you. We never came and we are not going. You see, this is why it is hard to explain certain things to you. You know it inside, but you have to consciously be aware of it. You have to know it consciously, and when you do know it, there will be no necessity to keep repeating the same cycle. No beginning, no end, only now. Infinity; this is how it is. This we know. Your vibrational energy will help you to know. No necessity to reason or try to apply logic. You know or you don't know; it is very simple. This is development.

Many species are trying to learn like you are. Many species do not understand. We do not understand all. Energy has decided to create itself in many forms. Your mind would wish to separate those forms. It is incorrect. The cycle will continue within all forms, within every physical living form. Energy chooses where to reside and how to reside. I know you understand the theory, but I also know you cannot possibly know. Your science is advancing fast, in what you call time, as you are aware there is no right and there is no wrong, but you are advancing also.

If you do not return to the cycle, it is your choice. If you return to this cycle, it is also your choice. It is likely you will not, but it will be your choice. You find it difficult to know that you have already made that choice. This is the now. You find it difficult to understand, within what you call time, how you could have already made that choice. You have made that choice. Again, you cannot understand this. I am telling you this in the best way I can tell it you. I do not know any other way to say it. It is the truth. It is two different worlds from your conditioned understanding.

This is what you are preparing for. It is metaphysical. You cannot control this flow. There is no control. The most important thing for you to feel is the real love from the source. The most important thing for you to do is to know yourself. When you know yourself, your world will change like you cannot imagine. It is impossible for you to imagine this whilst you are in the physical form. It is the reason you chose it so you could not imagine it. Again, this sounds strange to you. Why would I choose something I could not imagine? It was necessary for your cycle to do this. It is necessary every time for your cycle to do this.

You call us your higher self. This is correct, but it is not correct in an egotistical view. It is one. It is the same. We are the same as you. We are you. Again, the same words. You need to be guided. We are not brainwashing you. You need to be guided.

We need to be guided. You need to be reassured. Your conditioning needs reassurance, always. It is unnecessary for us. Reassurance does not exist. We know. Our questions about the source are much clearer than your questions. We also learn from you.

You do not need to look for proof. Many forms have given you many messages. There is a lot of truth in this information, but you do not need to confuse yourself. It is so simple. In your physical world it is so complicated. In their physical world it is also complicated, many emotions, many dynamics, many battles occurring, metaphysical battles. You are only as good as the information you receive, and often that information is incorrect. You are protected because you are looking towards the source, always. The source is pure. It is pure love. It is white; it is clear; it is crystal. We too are looking towards the source. Without this guidance, you would be totally confused.

You must know; you must know yourself. Know thyself. Your Christian religion told you this; it is common. Not just in the Christian religion it is common. Know thyself, and you will know.

Physical battles have no consequence other than to change the direction of the energy, the frequency, to force it into a different position of thought, of creativity, of imagination. Everything you are doing is correct. You will raise your vibration. Your world is raising its vibration now, many.

To say that you will leave is an incorrect statement once again. You are not going anywhere. To say that you will change is correct, but you are not leaving anything. There is nothing to leave. It's your interpretation, your conditioned interpretation, you are going to leave to go somewhere else. This is not going to happen. There is nowhere to go. It is only one place in the metaphysical world. This is why we can be anywhere in an instant, in the moment, because we are everywhere in an instant, in a moment, in a moment in what you call time. So there is nowhere to leave, to go to. Your interpretation of time is ridiculous. You will understand this. Vibrational energy, that is what you are. Do not create stories around us and confuse yourself. We are you.

Your mind is fighting very hard now to retain its position. Your consciousness is very aware. It is also fighting very hard to raise your vibration.

Freedom is what you think it is. Freewill is also what you think it is, but you also think you can lose it. This is impossible. You will imprison yourself with your own thoughts, your own imagination. You cannot lose it. You can contain it, and neither can any force ever take it from you. Again, this is impossible. You can trap it, but not, not for eternity in what you call time. It is all the same cycle, the same process. Once again, the same information. You are free; you have always been free, and you will always be free. It is simple.

<u>Session 21 - 22/06/2022</u>

You are here again to know the truth. It is good that you do this. Did you ever wonder how from all of the chaos that you create, there is always something at the end of it, it is good? How can this be possible? This is the uniform, the pattern. When you create, you create for a reason. When you use your form of energy, you use it for a reason. It's not important that you know that this is the reason, but you do. Out of the chaos and the madness that you create, there is always something good at the end of the process, something positive. Did you ever ask yourself how it is possible? Yes, you will say it is by coincidence. There are no coincidences.

It is good that you join us again. It is good that you join your higher selves again. It is good that you want to know. We know it is tiresome for you. This is a situation that is created through matter. To communicate is a process.

There is little you can do to change what is happening in your world. It is insignificant to your journey; it is a tiny part of the process. Again, I repeat to you the same thing. Your awareness of truth, of God, in your words God, the source, your awareness of this will set you free. You are already free, but you do not know it. We know the love from the source. You too, you know also.

Do not contaminate your physical life with the metaphysical world. Do not cross them. It will only confuse you *(1)*. What you know is a tiny part of what is real. You must separate; you must try to separate to understand. You will never fully be able to separate whilst you are a physical form, but you can separate.

We stop many from communicating with you *(2)*. It is a pure channel. Purity is important. When I say we stop, it is not like you think. We cannot force; we can only explain to them. The decision is theirs; it's not ours. But we think it necessary to encourage. We cannot control. It is impossible for us.

You are correct to ignore what is taking place in your world, in your physical world. I tell you before, it is insignificant. The real world, metaphysical world is infinite. So many opportunities for you to choose; so many directions for you to go. Your conditioned thoughts have confused you in what you call time, which is necessary. It is a necessary process of confusion to create awareness, to move up, to move higher with self, self-realisation. Again, the message is the same. Know thyself, self-realisation. When you know yourself, you will know all. It is one. It is necessary to experience the love from the source. You can feel it in here… I know *(3)*.

Each person, each consciousness, each soul in your world, you created them, and they created you. You are the same thing. Many, many giving out frequencies everywhere, energy, confusion, chaos. This was deliberate. You allowed it to roam, to go free with its thought process. You allowed this to happen for a reason—because it is all one, it is us, it is you—but you allowed it to go freely within chaos for a defined reason. Now it will slowly come together back to the source. Of course, the chaos exists. It exists for a reason. But it is correct. This is of little concern to you. You could say in your words it is manageable, deliberately manageable, meant to be managed. You must stop trying to separate this from yourself; it is you. There will be a balance again, a balance of energy, a balance of minus and plus, of positive and negative. It will balance again. Again, little concern of yours, the process is taking place.

You cannot stop the intrigue of others. They are you. You cannot prevent them asking questions. They will. But this is necessary for this part of you, which is them, to awaken, so you must help. By helping them, again—I tell you again—you are helping yourself; it is a natural process. But you are not responsible for them. You do not owe them anything. This is different. There is no debt; it doesn't exist. You created an illusion of debt in your world. It doesn't exist.

You must relax now. It is so simple. There is only the love and the light and the peace of the source. It is all that the source knows. It is bright. You have always known this. It is the very reason you are on this journey. You are attracted to the source as we all are, as all life is. You do not need to fear; there is nothing to fear. Fear is your creation; it is part of your world, of your world of many people, of you; another distraction, another tool you use to distract yourself. There is no need to fear. It is a powerful energy, an unnecessary energy. Unnecessary in the metaphysical, not unnecessary in the physical; it is different. You do not need to fear. You are getting closer.

Notes:
1. *He will tell us later, session 45, to hold two places, one physical and one metaphysical, and to bring them together to understand what is currently happening in the world, and that we have the capacity to do this. We have learned a lot since...*
2. *At the beginning of the meditations in the cave, John felt and saw presences, including a 'Little Grey'... These presences have indeed disappeared.*
3. *John actually feels in an ecstatic state during transmissions.*

<u>Session 22 - 24/06/2022</u>

The energy in your world changed today; you felt it *(1)*. It will change consistently now, and constantly. It is no concern of yours. There will be many changes in your world in what you call time. Your only goal is to understand yourself. This is the key to your understanding of everything, because we are all connected. By understanding yourself, you will understand all. The moment is all that is important, but the moment can be changed. The moment of everything, every action, every emotion, all of time, is only a moment.

The source will guide you, always. Without this direction you are lost. We too are lost. You must feel love from the source as much as you possibly can. You must see it in everything, in everyone, in every living thing, in everything you created. You must look within the structure to see the source.

You have a good understanding of DNA, of science. You have enough to understand, to see, to know. I keep telling you it is simple; it is not complicated. And I know you feel it is complicated when you are living outside of this channel.

The frequency between us and you has to be pure. Again, there is a defined pureness. It has to be defined, otherwise it can be contaminated. It is made up of vibrations. You can raise the vibration of your machine, your body. You can also prevent your mind interfering with your consciousness, your soul—your words. All the physical creations out there are formed from energy. That includes you. When you raise your vibrational energy, you raise your awareness of this. Again, it is simple, in practice it is difficult. You merely need to understand yourself as a form of energy to understand everything, energy from the source, clear, pure.

Creation of life and physical matter comes from the source. It is technology; it is God's technology, your words God, the source. You choose to be whatever you wish to be, wherever you wish to be, when you wish to be. But at the same time you are connected to all energy forms. It is a sequence, although your science would not say this. They would say it was erratic. It is not. It is formed specifically and very precisely; it is a natural occurrence.

Your emotional capacity to create diversions for yourself, your mind, many different emotions, the strongest emotion is fear. You would say minus; it is not. It is a balance, a necessary balance.

We do not fully understand the source ourselves. We only know the power that is created from the source. You feel it yourself as we do. You are in awe of this energy. You are drawn to it like a moth to a flame, always. This is your life. You are a part of this energy as we all are, as every living thing is, as every creation is, as every physical creation is, as every mental thought is. It is the same thing.

Although we know we must join the source—we are like you—we have not. But we are metaphysical. We are not physical, but our journey is the same. Just because we understand the technology doesn't mean we understand the source. We, like you, want to learn more; we want to advance. The cycle never ends.

Life can be created; physical life can be created in any form, by you, by us, which makes it irrelevant. Your journey is one moment. I know you cannot understand one moment, but you will. Infinity is one moment of eternal lasting.

I have given you so much information, and yet you think it is too simple. That is because of your conditioning. You yearn for complication. You crave for data, information. As a species you never stop craving for data and information. Data and information is useless without wisdom. You cannot apply. They go hand in hand together. Data on its own has no meaning; it is futile. It is merely a tool to create wisdom. Knowledge, data, the human species has a yearning for so much information, creating highly technological, biologically technological machinery to entrap itself within its own creation, when really the answer does not lie within the creation of the human species. It lies within the consciousness of self. This is pure; this is a pure emotion of thought. This is the source, the love of the source, all-encompassing.

I would prefer not to give you detail, but I can if you wish. It is totally unnecessary. Names, you give everything names. It is an emotion. I told you before, you build a story around it; you entrap yourself within it. It is totally unnecessary. This is what you do. This is what your mind does, your ego. If I give you the information, what will you do with it? You will, you will set out or attempt to prove, to prove I exist. Why would you do that? You know I exist. I am the same as you. Once you've proven this, what you do with that information is nothing. There is nothing you can do. You already know. So what is the purpose? Would it satisfy your intrigue? Would this work? No, it would not. Would it satisfy your thirst for wisdom? No, it would not.

You are receiving wisdom. There is no necessity to confuse you. It is clear. This information will be useful to some; they will find you. Remember: like attracts like; opposites repel. A simple force of a magnet tells you this *(2)*. This is energy; this is the electromagnetic field. You are changing. You understand more. There is much, much more to understand, to know.

You are never going to be isolated when you can feel the source. You felt the source all of your lives, both of you. You feel isolated. You make yourself feel isolated. It is your ego; it is your mind. You will never be isolated—it is impossible—isolated from what you treasure the most, the source. It will never occur. We never leave you. We are part of you.

The human form is incredibly spiritual—in your words. It has no cut off; it has no stop in its relentless journey to understand the source. Not all are like this. Not all physical creations are like this. It is relentless in its journey to understand. When you become aware, there is no stop. It is impossible. No going back; it is also impossible. I know you have tested this many times. So yes, the human form is special within what you call the universe. This we do know, but it is still the same. We do not know that it is special to the source. We do not separate the source. We are one of the same, part of. But we do know the human consciousness, and we do know it thrives to be nearer to the source. This is our interest in the human form, the human consciousness. We consider it to be faith, relentless, blind, nevertheless, tremendous energy forging forward all the time. This is how we can see it. Many species are not the same as this. They are controlled by their own minds, their own egos. They are stayed; they are fixed. The human form keeps going. You would say you chose this form in desperation to understand. Desperation is not the correct word to use; you chose this form to understand. It is simple. The energy created by the human form is immense. In the face of adversity—your words—it is non-stop forward. No matter how they feel, they keep surging forward; you keep surging forward. You cannot destroy the energy from the source—it is impossible—and you have it within, as all things do. It is deeply hidden among many, so far deep they cannot see it, but not you.

You have to relax. Remember, fear is your created illusion. There is nothing to fear.

Notes:
1. *I've never been so tired as I was this morning when I got up. I wanted to go back to bed, for no reason. Tina, John as well as other friends felt exactly the same.*
2. *It seems to us that there is a scientific ambiguity here, because our science has determined that the positive and negative of a magnet attract each other.*

Session 23 - 26/06/2022

Many words have been spoken. I have told you before, the spoken words that you use are not an ideal form of communication. Communication is emotion, frequency. It is given out in the form of a frequency. Your words can be confusing. This is why this channel has to be clear for the words to form in a correct manner. It has to be clear, otherwise the meaning is lost. The meaning is the most important part of the communication, the feeling, the emotion. This is knowing.

Knowing is far more important than your emotions that are given out. Knowing is not thinking you know. Knowing is knowing, knowing the source within. The difference between your mind and your consciousness, your mind does not know, your consciousness knows; it feels. This is the deciding factor for you. You have both, I would like to say at war with each other, but this is not correct. Harmonisation is the ability to discern between the two, to understand, to know, to know the reason why you have to go through this process. Enlightenment is the ability to be able to separate and understand the reason, to know the reason.

Opposing forces that meet as one, this is the technology from the source. You would like to say that one is minus and one is plus, one is positive, one is negative. But it is only one, the source. The source is bright light. It is neither minus or plus, positive or negative. It is neither one. It is one. It is a different energy. You ask the question, is it positive? It is not. It is a different energy. It is everything. I answered your question, and again it is difficult for you to understand this. It is all energy. So again, I have no words to explain the energy of the source. In your world there are no words to explain this. Your scientists didn't discover this. They don't understand it. For them there always has to be one or the other. It is impossible for them to understand. There can only be one, one moment, one time, one energy.

You may ask whatever question you like to ask, but it does not mean to say that I can explain it to you in the words, the simple words that you use. It is impossible. Your words are limited. Your emotions are not. Your frequencies are not limited. Your words are very limited. So once again, your mind and your words can be futile. Your emotions, your feeling is never this way.

All forms of energy exist in different ways, some physical, some metaphysical. We are metaphysical, but it is the same. There are many forms of energy, infinite, at different levels of understanding. It is true to say that some forms of energy would wish to apply only control. This is through fear. The most powerful form of energy that exists is fear. But, of course, love from the source is completely different. I do not term this a form of energy; I term it the creation of energy. It's different. This we need to understand as you do. Although it is an incredible energy, it is also the creation of energy, the creation of all energy, all forms of energy, physical and metaphysical. You would ask, where, how, what? Well, with the source we do not know. We cannot answer. We know it exists, but, like you, we cannot answer.We can only apply what we know. It is impossible to apply what you do not know.

You must create, use your imagination. You might say experiment, but it is not an experiment. You must acquire wisdom through knowledge which knowledge is already inert; it is inside you. You must understand the structure; we too.

You have set out on a serious journey. Historically it has not been so serious for you. It is necessary. Laughter does come from the source. It's a very powerful energy, but we find it necessary to focus, to focus on all of the questions that you need answered. We do not like to complicate, especially with words. It is the most serious journey you will ever make, and you will continue to make. An endless journey, an infinite journey, but a serious journey, not a game, not an illusion, real.

The part of our universe that we understand is ever expanding, many creations every day, outwardly expanding. We are all responsible for the expansion and the creation of physical matter, in one form or another. We are all responsible for the expansion of our universe, of which there are many universes, of which we know little about. Infinite, all in one moment, one time, many forms, physical and metaphysical, hand in hand together as one. You will visualise expansion in a physical form; it's not. You cannot visualise the expansion because your mind will try to rationalise this. It is impossible. Once again, you are trapped. Your scientists talk about the expansion of the universe as though they understand it. On a physical form they do, but they do not understand it. It is metaphysical; it is not physical, although it is both. You see, it is so difficult for you to understand this with your mind, and you will always apply your mind to try and understand it. When you leave your body, it will be clear.

But you are here, so you have to experience both physical and metaphysical. You have to experience both because they are the same thing. You are driven by a desire to know. There are no secrets. You can know, but you cannot know unless you understand. If your capacity to understand is limited, then you cannot know. But it will not always be limited. This is what you are preparing for. The question is, how much will you understand? The answer is enough, enough to know. You are understanding more and more, and ultimately, we will all understand everything in a moment. And sometimes, we do as you do. That moment is pure, clear, fulfilling.

What an incredible journey for you this is. You have worked very hard to get to this point. All and every are experiencing a journey of some kind. We are happy to share with you our journey. We are sharing our journey with you. Your journey is our journey; it's everyone's journey, the journey of everything. It is the same.

You must look more towards natural processes in what you have created in your world, natural processes, what your world would call natural things. Of course, your science is trying to play with natural things. They are playing with natural things. The purpose is for control through fear. But they will not succeed. They will create turmoil, but they will not succeed. They are fighting against the wave. It is impossible. You must look more at natural resources, the source's creation, your creation, technology of the source.

Your religion has taught you to look at the source like a child looks at a parent. This is not correct. You must look at the source as though you are the same, because you are. You are a part. There is no higher. There is only one, the same. You can raise higher; there is no hierarchy within the metaphysical. No better. It's the same. You play with that one a lot in your world, hierarchy, your creation.

Enjoy the moment. Enjoy the moment before you exit and go out into battle again, once more, with yourself.

All matter is formed from your imagination through frequencies. Emotions are frequencies. They are the same thing. Through the imagination of all the different realms, universes, is formed so much matter, so many frequencies. Again, infinite, the journey is endless. But when you understand time, it is only one moment. Your time is an illusion created by you, created by your mind.

It is true to say that your creations are more productive for you when they come from your consciousness, but it is also important that your creations come from your mind. One is not better than the other. Both are necessary. Many are not ready for the creations that can come from the consciousness. Many are happy to create only from the mind.

I have told you before, what lies in the metaphysical is beyond your ability to understand, more to deal with. You would feel lost. Your reliance on your conditioning is immense on this world, more than you can imagine. You could not imagine. It is necessary for you to continue your journey in the physical, but it is also necessary for you to understand the metaphysical. Your application of your wisdom will only realise itself in the physical, but there are many things that you can do.

You must be aware that you did not miss anything. Your illusion of time makes you think you are missing something, but you did not. There is only the moment. You cannot miss something. You can rationalise and come to a conclusion, and this will take time in your world, but there is nothing to miss. Again, your conditioning tells you that time is ticking. It is not. It is a moment. It is the moment, the only moment. You fear missing something. You fear not doing something in the timescale you have given yourself. There is no time. It's your illusion, your fear, your created fear from your illusion.

You have created so many stumbling blocks in your life, deliberately to fall over them. Whilst this is necessary for your awakening, you must also be aware they are only your creation, your stumbling blocks in your mind. The path is clear. There are no blocks. You can run as fast as you like, or you can sleep. It's your choice. There is nothing that can stop you. You can stay here as long as you like, in what you call time.

Your intrigue of the metaphysical is intense. It is what I have said it is *(1)*. You wish to know more about us. There is little more I can tell you other than we are the complete opposite of what you believe is real. We can guide you; I can guide you; you can guide yourself. You are guiding yourself. You have to move away from your conditioning to understand what is spoken here. You will apply it, always, your conditioning. You will apply, and it will confuse you. You have to recreate our world with your imagination, a new word for you, imagination. Frequency, this is the only way you will understand the metaphysical. You have to start at the beginning which is also the end, which is also the moment. You have to start to recreate without the interference of your conditioned life, to build a new story. To understand us correctly, this is what you have to do.

Your story is so basic, conditioned, controlled by you for a reason, the reason you are here. You are constantly looking for errors, errors from us. You may think they are errors, but we only give you the information that we know. There is no reason for us to give you any other information. How could we? Why would we? But your inquisitive mind will question everything. This is not bad. There is no bad. For you it is necessary. For us it is a waste of energy.

You have important things to learn; your journey has just begun. There is so much more. We too have to learn from you. We learn from every living thing and every metaphysical thing. We choose to learn. We choose to acquire wisdom. You too, you chose the path of learning. Your life cycles were orientated around this path of learning, of growing, of experiencing all and everything in one moment. But remember, that moment can be changed. Although it is written, it can be changed. This is hard for you to understand. It is your choice. One can change; billions can change—it is the same thing—in an instant.

You can feel the energy now. This is your creation. This is our creation. You can see it.

Your patience sometimes fails you. It's getting better. You must understand that you need to know self. You need to understand self. Without knowing self, you will not know. By knowing self, you will know everything; every individual you will know, because they are the same as you. I repeat again the same thing. It seems endless to you as though you are waiting. You are not. It is a moment of realisation. It is an instant. There is no time, and that moment is infinite, eternal. So your impatience is your creation from your mind.

You will not do yourself an injustice by being an active member of the physical world; it is part of the process. Do not think you have raised your consciousness, that you are not worthy to take this role *(2)*. You have to take this role. You have to integrate. It is part of the process. But be aware of all. This is the only thing you have to do. Be aware; understand. You have spent many hours in what you call time attempting to understand. You have got very far with this. There is much more; it will come. It is simple, but it is only simple when you know.

We do not make mistakes in the way you would term mistakes. Our words are chosen. We will see, we will see when you write. Your ego is never failing you. We are not challenging you; it is not how we are. You wish to challenge us. We do not understand this. We do not relate to it. There is no answer for you. We are you and you are us. By challenging us, you are challenging yourself. Why would you do that? It is in your conditioning, simply in your conditioning. But, again, necessary for your journey. You have always challenged everyone and everything. The other energy in this room does not challenge. His conditioning has taught him to love, to care, to associate, to be kind. But, again, it is conditioning. Both necessary, both opposing.

You must relax, both of you.

Notes:

1. *John had planned that evening to challenge him, desperately looking for the slightest mistake on his part. In real time during the session, he believed he made an error of word choice…*
2. *John and I have tended to take a certain step back from society, often straining to participate (social life, business…).*

Session 25 - 29/06/2022

The circle of life is the cycle of life. You use the word past lives. There is no such thing as past. It is in one time, one moment, at the same time. Your illusion of time uses words like past and future. One moment, one time, you have to use your imagination to understand this. It is necessary that you know how this works. A complete process instantly in one moment. This, for you, has been a stumbling block for a long time in what you call time. For you to know, it is necessary for you to understand.

All is accessible, all information is accessible. Just like a computer needs a command for you to extract the data within, billions and billions of data, you need to give a command, a correct process for you to understand, to collect the data within. It is the command that is important, the understanding of the process.

Eternal is the circle. Infinite is the circle. Right around and back to the beginning every time. The beginning is in every part of the circle. Every point is a beginning; every point is an end. Round and round and round, beginning, end, beginning, end, consistently, beginning, end, and infinite, this is the way it works. If you can rationalise from your conditioning, then you will understand a part. You will not understand all. Every point is a beginning, and every point is an end in a linear circle. In a sphere, it is highly formed with beginnings and endings of a multitude, of an infinite amount of possibilities in one, one sphere. Yes, it is incredible information for you to visualise such. This is reality. All your matter is made up of circles, protons, neutrons; you would call them, minus, plus. Circles, they are circles, spheres, coming and going; you would say erratically, but it is not erratic: it is uniform; it is precise; it is specific to you. The channel is clear today. Linear is a circle; infinite is a sphere. There is a difference. Together as one in one time, one moment, joining. And, of course, you can change that moment. You can change everything. It is your choice. But you always make the journey again, and you always start again from the beginning. And where you end you will start; it is the same point.

Imagination from your mind is the same as your imagination from your consciousness. It is one. But the energy is applied differently. One is not less important than the other, merely the application is different. One can become the other if your mind allows it to, which often it does not, so the energy is wasted; it is futile because of lack of application. The consciousness does not need application; it is automatic. So, one has to make a journey. It has to cross a bridge. To have its worth, it has to cross a bridge, whereas the other does not need to cross a bridge; it is an automatic application. So it is far easier for you to create with your imagination through your consciousness than it is to create with your imagination through your mind. But both are the same. I hope that clears that up for you. When you leave your body, you create with your imagination through your consciousness, because you are not physical anymore. There is no sense to apply your conditioning.

You have all the tools. I give you the tools. You must try to practice. I know you will find this hard whilst you are in a physical form, but it is possible to experience such. It is possible to leave your body and experience these things whilst you are still physical. Most people that do this do not understand where they go to and what they are doing. Hence chaos once more. But if you have an understanding of this before you experiment, then your application will be better, clearer. There are techniques you can use to create an out of body experience, but in reality, it is from within you. It is your will, your need, your want, your desire. This will create what you are looking for. Techniques are merely your mind-created gadgets; they are not necessary. You do not need a crutch anymore. You do not need gimmicks, names, brands. Not necessary for you.

It is only very recently, in what you call time, that you have come to the understanding of what the imagination really is, the frequency, the power, the energy. You are starting to realise how insignificant what is happening in your world is to you. It took a while. You are starting to realise that outside of this little world you created is something far, far deeper and far greater than this occurrence. This is good. It is good that you are starting to understand how insignificant it is.

Do you not think this process is occurring within other universes? Of course it is. It is an accumulation of universal energy. It is an accumulation of many energies that creates this position. It is necessary. You now are starting to feel the excitement of what lies in the metaphysical world. I know this, and it is exciting. It is still exciting for us also. We are still creating like you. You are starting to realise how insignificant your conditioning is, how ridiculous it is. We are fortunate enough to know this. Without knowing, it matters not what you create on the physical world you live in; you will always be empty. Whether you create power, wealth, whatever you create is insignificant to knowing. And your soul as you term it, your consciousness will be empty, yearning to know. It is the only thing that is important. Know thyself. Know.

Your journey is bright. It is filled with excitement, one after another, one experience after another of excitement. It will get easier for you now. You have made it very hard for yourself. You have made it incredibly hard for yourself, but it will get easier now. Knowing is fulfilment, contentment, peace, love of the source. And you must help others also, because you are helping yourself, always. You cannot coerce; this is incorrect. But you can guide; you can help; you can direct; you can point; you can suggest. They will come to you for help, but you must be careful how you help, in what way you help, how you apply the frequency of help. Again, it is not so simple as you think it is. You must analyse. You must look at their situation, their meaning, their reason, their position. You must analyse them. How could you help them unless you understand them. You must feel what they are feeling. You cannot intervene. You cannot try to take control of their lives thinking you are helping them. You will not help them; you will hinder them; you will hinder yourself. Help, you have to analyse this. It is not as simple as you think it is.

Your mind is clearer today. This is good. It's perfect. You must move forward now. Stay relaxed and move forward.

<u>Session 26 - 02/07/2022</u>

Knowing makes it very easy to apply the formula, to create. Not knowing makes it difficult. This is your conundrum. Because we know, we can apply. It is only a formula, a process. What you have created in your world is an illusion. And what you continue to create is based on that illusion. It is based on your fear. Your fear if you don't create is part of the process. So, for us it is much different than it is for you. We know if we create an illusion, which we do, we do create an illusion, but we know it's an illusion. You do not know. So there lies the confusion.

Money is your creation, your illusion, your fear. Your fear of not having money forces you to create money. In the metaphysical there is no necessity for money. You created this system, and you live within it. It is a cycle of fear. Your journey is to understand it. You will not understand it unless you participate in it. So, the question is, is it wrong or is it right to want to create money *(1)*? For you, it is right, although there are no wrong or right. It is right within your illusion. It is right for you to participate in all the aspects of the illusion you have created. This is the only way you will understand why you created it in the first place. There is no wrong or right. Again, I tell you the same. There is no judgment. There is only experience, only creation. It is important for you to know self to understand this. This is your development, your growth, your experience. You may think whilst you are in your illusion that money is important, based on the fact you created that illusion. But, of course, it is not. But it is necessary for you to participate; that's the very reason you are here in this world. And every one of you is at a different stage in your journey of understanding. Everything happens for a reason. Do not think it does not.

You are fully aware of the consequences of the creation of finance, good and bad. The controlling energies in your world are getting more powerful. It is not really a concern of yours, but it will have an effect. It will change direction. This process has been in flow for a long time in what you call time. Very little has changed with the type of energy that is projected. It is not new. It is also necessary. Within a three-year time period of what you call time, your world will be unrecognisable to you. But, again, it is not a concern for you. The origin of the control is from the fear of man, from your species, fear, the fear of not being in control. Their own creation, your own creation.

We do not intervene. We cannot; we know it is incorrect. We cannot; we will not. We can guide; we can tell you what we know. We cannot intervene; this will damage us. There are other energies that are interfering also within the consciousness of a man's mind. They are also controlling energies. We can also advise them, what they are doing, and how they are doing it. And we do. But the bridge between the mind and the consciousness is never always easy to cross, nor to understand.

Your focus is important. You must stay focused. It can all change in one moment. When the vibration is lifted, it can change in one moment, a cycle. We can see the future, in what you call future, because it has already happened. It is happening now. But it can change. Your creation of energy, your frequency can change all. You can merely start at another position, and start again, and end at the same position. It is like a dial. It can start and stop at any point you like, over and over again. The formation of physical and mental is for you to decide as it is the same for us.

Control takes its effect from fear. You create the fear and allow it to control. It's very simple. Maybe not so simple in practice, but very simple in reality. We are beyond this. We do not understand it in our world. We know. So we apply what we know, always. You apply what you think you know, and you apply what you know: chaos, confusion, madness. But also necessary for your journey. So, there is no right, there is no wrong; there only is what you apply. At the end of that journey, there is wisdom and knowledge from within. So you must experience all and everything.

You cannot experience if you do not know yourself. It is impossible. How would you know you even had an experience if you do not know yourself? You are experiencing constantly many things. You are experiencing things you are not even aware of. You must continue to experience, physically and metaphysically. You must continue your journey. You must continue to create, to cross the bridge and to cross it back again, over and over again until eventually you will only make one choice, a precise direction. You will go in a precise direction knowing the uniformed pattern exists, and you will recognise this. You chose this journey to make consciously; you chose. And you consciously chose to forget all of the other journeys you made, otherwise you could not experience the journey that you chose if you had kept all of those memories.

Allow yourself to understand. It is far simpler than you think it is. Allow yourself to know, to feel. You are protected by the source. It lies within. It lies within all and every. You are protected. You cannot make a wrong choice. It is impossible. I think your understanding of this is getting clearer.

Everything is relevant to you. You will see many things; you will hear many things; you will smell many things; you will participate in many things. It is all relevant to your direction, your chosen direction. Remember you created it. You placed it in a position for you to recognise it. You placed it there so on your journey you could relate to it. It would ignite you. So all and everything around you is irrelevant. This is why you are able to recognise something. This is why you can relate to each other. You chose to meet. You chose this time in what you call time to meet, to recognise, to work on your journey *(2)*. There is an instant recognition within you. Symbols, processes, times, your creation time, you placed these symbols within the life you are in to recognise them. This is why they are so obvious to you. It is not an accident. It is meant by you from within yourself to remember. It is insignificant to remember the conditioning. It is significant to know, to remember, to understand the process.

You must relax, and enjoy what you have created, explore what you have created, experience what you have created.

Notes:
1. *John and I deliberately put ourselves in a particular situation in relation to money. Both withdrawn from professional life, we care little about it, not that we have plenty of it, quite the contrary, but because we have confidence in life and know that our basic needs will be filled. But in the cave, we are urged to participate, to create again. Hence our questions about the relevance of recreating money and its compatibility with our spiritual journey...*
2. *Beyond everything that surrounds us and conditions our lives, there has been this innate recognition between John and me, from the beginning. And, for both of us, special circumstances have taken place, an irrepressible momentum coming from within that has led us to find each other as neighbours here, him far from his country, and me far from my ties.*

Session 27 - 04/07/2022

I see you have concluded there is little more I can tell you. This is your fantasy. Your journey has only just started. There is lots more I can tell you, but there is lots that you will not understand. I can give you an insight, but that is all. You will never fully understand *(1)*.

You will continue to feel your pain. You must remember you chose to feel this pain *(2)*. Pain is an illusion. It is your illusion. It is not just the pain of the people you feel the pain for, it is yours also. It is yours; it is theirs; it is ours; it is everyone's pain. It is the same thing. It is an emotion; it is frequency. You must remember when you feel the pain, it is only an illusion, your illusion. We feel the pain, and we know what it is. You do not know. It's difficult, I know, for you to separate the two; you feel it so deep it cuts you like a knife. But it is only your illusion. Pain in the way you interpret pain does not exist. It is not real.

You must allow others to go through their process. You cannot force change or interfere with their journey. This will inhibit your growth. You can only advise them on the facts, the process, guide them. You cannot interfere. You cannot interfere with even what you consider to be the closest, the people you have chosen to exist with, for a reason. And the reason is equally from you as it is from them. It is not them; it is you also. It is the same. Yes, I know, it hurts. You chose these people for a reason, and when you feel the pain, this is the reason. It is correct. It is necessary; it is necessary to understand the process. So it is not as you would term bad. It is good. It is growth for you and for them. It is real. Yes, you understand now. Now you are in a place that is clean. It's clear. But out there you get confused with your own journey, your own emotion, your own output, your own creation. You get unclear. You must learn; you must learn to separate, to analyse, to adapt, a process, simply a process. It does not mean you are without emotion; it does not mean you are without love. The only love that is important in your life is the love from the source. It's purer. It's pure energy.

Do not act like a child with a child mentality of good and bad, of judgment. It is ridiculous. But you will revert back to this again and again. Your childlike view will give you comfort. It is not real comfort; it is an illusion of comfort. This is the process. It is also correct, yes. How can it be correct when the feeling is so painful? But it is correct. It is correct for you to analyse and understand why it is occurring, how it is occurring. In every situation it's different. It has an array of emotion attached to it, of frequencies. You would not even understand how many, more than you could even imagine, or see, or know. The complexities you have built in the world you live in are intense, incredible. But the answer is simple, so simple it is sitting under your nose, and you do not even see it, such a simple solution to such a complex problem, which you chose. We do not have this problem you have. We do not even understand the word problem. We have to interpret the word for you. We know, but we need to know more; just like you, we need to know more. We are the same. We are one. But we need to know more, like you need to know more.

You are often put in a situation where you can feel fear. It is also necessary for you to feel the fear, but it is necessary for you to know that it is only fear, a feeling, an emotion, a frequency. Once you are aware of that, it cannot hurt you or stop you. You are protected. You can adapt yourself accordingly to this, and you can eradicate it. Again, simple, harder in practice for you and your conditioned life, much harder for you to apply the principle, the process, but it is necessary that you do. Many will no longer feel the fear, and the outcome is irrelevant to you. It may be relevant to others, but it becomes irrelevant to you, because you eradicated the fear. It's like a counterbalance of frequency of energy. You are pure energy. It's what you are, pure energy from the source. It is the same message, but spoken in a different way. It may appear repetitive to you, but it is not. Each and every time you will learn more. You will note more every time until eventually you will know. You will know enough. You will never know all until you are metaphysical.

You cannot force your view. You cannot force what you know. You cannot control with what you know. It is not pure. It has no beginning or no end. It has no reason. It is impossible for your journey to do this. You must allow, allow others to search for their freedom, for their wisdom. You can guide, and by doing this —again I tell you—you will help yourself, as you will help them, because it is the same.

In what you call time, your journey has only just begun, both of you. Do not think that you know it, because you don't. You know enough, but enough is a fraction, a tiny fraction. You know enough to know what is occurring in your small world has no significance on your consciousness, your soul as you call it. You know this. For you in this time, what you call time, that it is enough. Of course, there is much more. It is what you call positive. But of course, positive and negative are necessary. Plus and minus are both necessary. They are the same thing from the source. If you want to apportion blame, then you are to blame for what is occurring as we all are to blame. But of course, there is no blame; it does not exist. A process.

The human species, the human brain is so creative. For us, it is incredible to see how creative you can be. In every circumstance that arises, your mind will create a solution very quickly to pacify your consciousness. It is incredible. The reality of this: it is not real. But it is so creative as too is your consciousness, so creative and so pure and so connected to the source. We had to work very hard to be at the point you are at now with your connection to the source. It is incredible that you can do this. And yet it is also incredible to us how you want to keep fighting yourself. This we do not understand. We understand the process you endure. We do not understand why you would do this. We understand it is necessary for you to do this, to experience and to raise your vibration, but we do not understand why you would do it. It is almost as though you have to do it as part of your process. You see, to us we understand it, but we do not understand some of the things that the human species endures, as to why. You take the long road, and you dismiss the short road, always. You deliberately create a problem to solve it, always. And I am sure you enjoy the experience. When we create an illusion, it is knowing that we are going to participate in only enjoyment, no pain. When you create your illusion, you participate in pain, always. I think the terminology you use for this is masochist. But we do know that you are close to the source. And we ask, does this bring you closer? We do not know. This is our interest. We can only tell you what we know. There is no black or white in this. It is very clear, no mix of black and white. It is very clear; it is black or white. You seem to have more than black or white. You seem to have a mixture of many colours within yourself. We only have one or the other for our explanatory, our knowing. We know or we don't know. You seem to have something that sits in the middle. Once again, it's something we don't understand. We understand the process; we understand what you would term the end game, but, of course, the end is the beginning. And time doesn't exist; there is only one moment. So, this you don't understand yet, but you will. But we do not understand; we do not understand why you would put yourself through this. You choose to do it; you consciously choose to do it over and over again. You consciously choose not to remember, to do it again. Why? And we watch; we see. It is incredible. So, we don't know everything. We know process; we know emotion; we know frequency; we know the source. We can adapt; we can travel; we can create. But there are things we don't know.

You are feeling relaxed. You came here to feel this. This feeling is your consciousness at peace. This is something we feel always. This feeling is pure; it is from the source.

Notes:
1. *Some apparent repetitions (but in fact, always in a slightly different light), and their repeated confessions of not knowing or understanding everything would almost give John a little air of superiority, in an amused tone of course...*
2. *We often evoke with John the pain we feel in relation to some of our loved ones, which we see if not in a spiritual void, at least in an almost complete oblivion of their metaphysical existence. When we see them entangled in their difficulties, it is difficult for us to take a step back, to accept that they are in a different journey or in a different position, and often we suffer from it.*

Session 28 - 06/07/2022

Once again, you are making a challenge. You have applied your conditioned logic to form the solution *(1)*. It is not that simple to explain to you the metaphysical when you are participating in the physical. For you, the logic is simple. You are combining two worlds to make a solution. This cannot be done. You are making the situation complex. It is not. It is not so simple to do this, combining both. It is not possible to do this. They are different. Your creative illusions give you a false sense of knowing. We know. We do not know everything, but we know enough. So the answer to your question is not so simple for us to give you a reply. You will perceive this to be evasive. It is not. It is not so simple to cross-contaminate between the physical and the metaphysical. There are elements to what you say that are correct, but your logic does not make sense.

We, like you, are looking to know more about the source. You do have a connection to the source like we do, as one. We do not wish to confuse you, or interfere with your journey. There will be repercussions if we interfere. The same as if you interfere with anybody else's journey. So we wish you no harm. I am not trying to manipulate you. We can learn from you as you can learn from us. But it is not a simple question, not as simple as you may think it may be. We do apply what we know to make our lives simple, easy. You apply what you know to make your life difficult. This is what we know. We do understand that you go through cycles of difficulty. We do not. We can take any form we wish in a physical. But if we take a form, it is for a reason, otherwise we have no necessity to take a form. And often that reason is for our enjoyment, our pleasure. But we would not choose a form for pain. Again, pleasure, pain, it is an illusion. But it is felt. As an individual it is felt. So we choose. You, also, you choose. It is true to say that we are often intrigued why you choose so much pain, so we learn from each other. We want to know like you want to know, to understand more the source, the origin of all energy.

Whilst the principles of your religions are correct in many cases, they are also manipulated by yourselves, for control. We no longer look for control. We look towards the source for knowing as you do, as you choose to do, as you have chosen to do for many cycles in your life in what you call time. You will mistrust my words on the basis that I cannot directly answer your questions, but I can only tell you what I know. We do not wish to control you; we merely wish to learn, as one.

The question of higher self? We are one. You may consider in your conditioned world we are higher than you because we know. This is not correct. We are the same. It is only terminology. Again, conditioned terminology that would say we are your higher self. We are self; we are one. You would look at us as being wiser than you. We are not. We are the same. There is no higher; there is no lower. It is the same. So, we are again playing on words and perceptions, illusions. It is not real. You created the terminology higher self, because you want to believe that something exists outside of self that is better, bigger. If we can portray wisdom to you, you also to us, then neither is higher nor lower, but the same. Terminology is difficult to communicate.

It is only an expression, higher self, to explain a situation of experience. You are experiencing us. We, through the communication channel, are experiencing you. There is no higher or lower. There only is energy.

You are protected from the source because you are aware that the source exists. You cannot explain the source—we cannot—other than the creator of energy. We do not know if there exists other sources of energy. We do not think this is the case. We do not know. The infinite universe of many universes, we believe there is only one. We do not know. We do not mean to deceive you in any way. We know what we know. And, of course, it is all subject to one moment, one time which we know can be changed in an instant. And this you do not understand, neither can we explain it to you. Your science is trying to explain it, but they have not. So it is not so simple.

Communication in different languages, frequencies, emotions, are two tribes in separate dimensions. It's difficult. Words are incredibly difficult for us to express to you so you understand with your conditioned life what we are saying to you. Incredibly difficult, difficult for us to say, and sometimes, difficult for you to translate what we are trying to say to you. But we choose our words very carefully so as not to confuse. The conditions that are created within this cave, this area, are good for communication. It's a pure channel, and, of course, you know when you leave this cave, this area, you know that the channel becomes weak, until eventually it seems almost non-existent. You already know this. You already feel it. We, like you, have to create the correct condition for us to communicate with you. Often this is difficult. It is as difficult for us as it is for you.

The all-encompassing love, not your human created dependency but the all-encompassing love of the source, is the only thing we are trying to understand. As are you; it is the same thing. There is no necessity for us to manipulate. Our only desire is wisdom, more wisdom and more knowing, just like you. You have learned so much in a very short time, what you call time, but you have been learning for the whole of your existence—no beginning, no end, a process—we too.

Alleviate all your fears. There is no necessity for you to be scared of anything. The journey is filled with excitement. You choose to fill your journey with pain. We choose to fill our journey with excitement. We wish for all species, all life forms, all physical matter, all-encompassing of every physical creation to be at peace, one with the source. This is our wish. And if we help, we are helping ourselves on this journey. No right, no wrong. There is no right or wrong. But we know, given a certain direction that an energy will form and take, we know it is growth, expansion, creation, imagination. We know this, so we focus on this. We do not focus on the opposite of this, although they are both the same, from the source, from the creation of energy.

The source is infinite, no beginning, no end. You cannot understand this. If you want your question answered, you need to understand this. You need to know this. You need to understand, to know that there is no such thing as time. It does not exist; it is your creation. You need to understand all these things to answer your questions correctly, and you do not. I can only give you comfort that your journey is the correct journey. This is the best I can do.

There is no necessity for you to fear. I know you do not, but you will always challenge. Challenging takes you down a path to understand. It is your way, and we know every single intent meant by this. There is no deviation. And you will always be suspicious. It is part of the reason you challenge, but again, you chose to do this; you chose to be this; you chose to take this form for your journey to understand. It has always been your choice from the many cycles that you endure; it has always been your choice. This is the best I can do.

I will remind you again that you must participate. Do not be afraid of participating. Do not think that you know, because you don't. You must participate in the physical, and you must focus on the metaphysical. Both are the same. What is occurring has little relevance to you. Once again I tell you, it has little relevance to your journey. So you must participate. I know you are reluctant to participate based on the outcome of your physical world, but you must participate. It is important. It is important for your journey. You chose this.

You are having what you perceive to be your communications with us, an incredible journey. It is an incredible journey for you, and for us. There's not as many as you think that are in a point in their life where they can do this. There are others, but not so many as you think. This channel is open to all—all is one—it is open to anyone, but their conditioned life in your world does not allow them to make this step, to have this experience. You will try to explain this to many people; I'm afraid it will fall on deaf ears. But some it will not. Most will merely be intrigued, and then they will stop, because their conditioned life will carry them in the way it has chosen to carry them; in the way they have chosen it, it will carry them. Your world likes carnivals. It likes theatre. You would be theatre to most people. You would be a carnival; you would be a clown to most people within their created carnival. But to some you will not.

Carry on with the process. Carry on with the journey; you will see. But remember, one moment, no time.

<u>*Note:*</u>
1. Unfortunately we do not remember exactly what the question was; it must be said that we ask ourselves so many... I specify that no question is asked aloud in the cave. The Man In The Cave—we don't know how to call him otherwise—answers the questions that John and I ask ourselves before we go to meditate, or the questions we have in our heads. We don't even need to formulate them. But we were still wondering about his true identity as well as his real motivations... And always in the background, this memory of the 'Little Grey' taking John's hand in the cave, some time ago... I still think, following the lessons of the New Message, that these entities are experts in mental manipulation, hence once again a certain mistrust. And yet everything is so clear in this cave...

<u>Session 29 - 08/07/2022</u>

What do I mean when I say the channel is pure? It is a given set of principles that occurs in one moment. It is a process. Everything in the physical is made of molecules. Frequencies are made also of molecules, of atoms, constructed. So in a given situation, a precise situation, these have to form together to create a clear channel. This process is not easy to construct, because both parties have to construct it in the moment for it to work. When you are in the company of others, many particles, frequencies, are being transmitted, and your mind will interpret through your conditioning, feeling. This is where confusion lies. Cross-contamination is the particles not connecting correctly to form communication. You have experienced this process many times. So it is necessary to create the perfect connection through the creation of these particles, these atoms. And you do this as we do it, using the correct frequency.

Confusion and chaos within the process leaves you pondering on right and wrong. Of course, there is no right or wrong, but your mind tells you this. And then you initiate upon yourself judgment, and you create another frequency, a frequency of judgment. So many formations are created and felt in the form of energy. Most people are not aware that they are doing this. You are aware. Most people are in a state of total confusion, because they cannot rationalise the emotions they are feeling. They equate it to themselves when in reality it is not, it is everybody around them in that given situation. So it is important to create a clear channel of communication. When I say to you the channel is clear, this is what I mean. It is a clear channel created by us and created by you, as one. The conditions that you are in now are perfect to create a clear channel. There is interference, but very little. So when you are in the company of other energy forms like yourself, this is why when you leave the position you are in now, it can be very confusing to you, because you are receiving all of this information from everybody and everything around you. So you have to dissect the information, and analyse, and know where it is coming from. You have to know what you are feeling, and why you are feeling it, and who you are feeling it from, and what is their reason to transmit this information. Then you will understand, and you will know self. It is a simple process. It is not complicated, but your mind and your conditioning make it extremely complicated. It is for you to understand. Once you can understand this, you can apply it. You can apply it in so many ways in your life. It is not magic; it is a process. It is a scientific, technical process. It is not what you think it is. So, this is ours; this is yours; this is everybody's form of communication, or correct communication. We know this. You also know. Everybody knows. But they know deep inside, the part of them they did not wake up. Your terminology has always been gut feeling. This is correct. And all of these frequencies are transmitting in one moment, in one time, in one point, one position.

And I say to you, it matters not what is occurring in the world for you. It will only change the position. It will not change the journey. This is position. You must also understand position, place, moment. You have experienced this, all of your cycles, the same process over and over again. Although you feel separated, you are not. You are not separated from anyone in your world. You are connected to everyone as we are connected to you, as all of these particles are connected, not isolated, connected. So you can feel one, and you can feel all at the same moment. Yes, so simple, in here. You do experience this at certain times in your life. In this life you are in, you may think something in a moment, and immediately in that moment another person will be with you, and they will say, "that is exactly what I was thinking", and there is no possibility in your conditioned world that this can happen. But this is the same process. This is what it is. You want an explanation for it; this is the explanation, the reality. One moment, no time. It's difficult for you to understand with your creation of time how this is possible. Time created by you confuses the issue. Remove the time, you will understand this moment.

We know that the source is the creation of all technology. We know that the source is the creation of all. We understand the process. You cannot deviate from the path. It is impossible. You cannot stop the motion, the growth, the expansion. It is impossible. You are expanding continually as we are, as everyone is, as the universe is, continually expanding and creating more molecules, more atoms, more frequencies, creating all of these things consistently, expanding. This is from the source. You cannot stop this. You cannot put it on hold. You cannot prevent it. It is a natural process—natural, the word natural is from the source—ever expanding, infinite. You must experience consciously this to understand it.

Your species are very good at creating theories. You create theories to prove facts, to prove this science. Your theories come from your imagination. Your imagination is capable of creating all and every theory that is available to create, to form a physical, to prove what you call a fact. You are moving so fast you don't even know it. The beginning, the end, it is the same; in any place you want to be, it is the same.

You do not call us to be here. We never left. We are always here. There is no here and there; it is the same point. So, in your conditioned life you would say, "Come to us." We never left. We are always here. For us it is another ridiculous request, but we understand, of course, what you are actually meaning. Again, the words are unimportant. The meaning is all important. This is how we have to translate from your conditioned world to understand what your request is. Your words are insignificant. And we are emotions and frequencies. Your creation of energy is what we know and understand.

Consciously apply. Consciously apply; you are aware, enlightened. It's another word you use. It gives the perception of better. There is no such thing as better. It does not exist. You see, your words create emotions that are incorrect, interpreted in a different way. And, of course, your mind takes over, your ego. This is not the way to move forward.

You are from a divine source of energy. Your energy within is pure. The minds of others would not think so. They create their own illusion. You must feel more. You must feel more, and recognise this at the moment, in the moment you do it, you must recognise this energy; you must acknowledge it. You do it consistently all the time, but subconsciously. You must learn to consciously know when you do it, when you receive it, when you transmit it. You must be aware of this, consciously aware, then you will grow very quickly. It is an easy process. You do have this ability, as do we all. This is applying, recognising consciously the transmission and the receiving of the frequencies, the energy.

There is nothing to fear. Fear lies within your illusion. Experience these energies, and recognise them from others and from yourself. With your understanding of this, the energy of wisdom will be created for you. The purest form of energy you can give to anyone is the energy received from the source. Whether they consciously or unconsciously receive this energy, it will change them, in the moment.

Session 30 - 09/07/2022

The terminology that you use is white noise. Today you can hear many frequencies coming within. White noise is all. Separation of frequencies is what you can hear today *(1)*. This is all forms of communication. You build many layers within yourself of complication. Information you receive and will be heard by you, when you are consciously aware of white noise—your terminology—when you are consciously aware, you can separate.

The frequency you use in here is a good frequency—good, termed in your words—a harmonious frequency. You can hear today three frequencies. You have separated them. We are one of those frequencies. Separation, you would term as tinnitus. It is not. It is specific, specific frequency. This is communication *(2)*.

All forms of communication, all living things, all non-living things in the physical world transmit frequency. The layers that you create confuse you. You build one after another, on top of each other, until eventually you are confused. By learning how to separate the layers, you will understand.

One frequency can carry an infinite amount of information. It is infinite. Whilst all the frequencies combined can do the same, it is only one, one from the source, separated by you, by us, by all living things as a form of communication, as a form of creation. As a specific receiver of information, you must learn how to separate. Frequency is also made of particles. It is correct that you are often in a state of confusion. It is a correct process for you to know. You have an understanding of this process, but it is only the beginning of the understanding. You can apply the process; you must apply the process. You cannot make mistakes; there is no such thing. You can only grow.

Man is trying, your species is trying to also understand the power of frequencies in a scientific capacity. They understand some; they do not understand all. Again, through their own fear, they would wish to use it as a weapon for control. You can inhibit this application on the basis of knowing how it works. And you do know. You have enough understanding of it to prevent manipulation with it. The very fact that we are here is an expression of your understanding. Creation of frequencies from all living things and non-living on the physical is a constant. In the moment it is infinite, ever expanding. We understand this process so therefore, we apply it.

We can be in the moment everywhere and anywhere in one given position, or in many, but there is still only one point. I know you are trying to understand this. It will be difficult for you. The answer will lie in your imagination. You cannot apply the practicalities of your conditioned logic to make this work. It is impossible.

Your thoughts around our existence are childlike, insignificant, based on your conditioning. Whilst you are half to the truth, it is not the truth. It is far simpler to understand in a metaphysical than it is in a physical, and contamination of the two will never achieve an understanding.

In the physical your imagination is formed in the center of your head. This is what you call the third eye, all seeing, all knowing, imagination. It is in the center between your eyes, is where the physical process begins. Your mystics for many years have talked about this process. They have applied many things that are not correct. It is merely a process, physical to metaphysical. You give it the name eye because, once again, you need to adapt a name, a brand, a meaning with a physical visual. It is not correct.

Every molecule within your physical body will react to every frequency that it receives. Action, reaction. You will create many forms of yourself in a physical form based on this reaction. They will change consistently. They will evolve. They will go from the start and back to the start—there is no beginning and no end, there is only one point—and you will continue to do this within one moment. And this is what you do. And you are affected by everything around you through frequencies. So your simple understanding of emotions in your world is far more complex. In our world it is natural for us to know this.

It is good that you challenge us. It is a way you learn. But you do not have to fear. The only thing we can gain—if gain is the correct word—from you, is to help ourselves by helping you. It is as simple as that. You are slowly learning this. You are learning to the point you will no longer challenge.

It is good that you are analysing situations. You are involved with other energies around you, other people. It is good that you are learning and feeling what they are throwing out into the world with their frequency *(3)*. It is good that you are able to rationalise and understand the meaning of their emotion based on their situation, based on their moment. This is the way you understand. It starts within. It starts within self-realisation. Self-realisation is expanded out to them to receive this information. It is good to receive. It is good to analyse. It is important you do this. The beginning of your journey.

You chose this journey. You chose to make this communication with us at this point in what you call time. Position can change always within a moment. The journey is infinite, eternal, never ending, one point, but position can change. This is different. And you are participating. It is necessary to tell you and to remind you there is no judgement. There is no right, there is no wrong way to participate. You will be drawn always to the source during your participation. The source is pure, so the decision will be correct. You may not think so at the time—your time—but it will be correct, because it is the energy of the source that you will be drawn to, always. So you must participate, and you must take pleasure in participating. No good, no bad, no judgments, so whatever the outcome is correct for you, you chose; you chose this journey to participate in the way you participate. So, relax and enjoy the process.

Notes:
1. *Upon entering the cave, John heard special tinnitus for the first time.*
2. *I specify that since the beginning of our meditations, and after having read a lot about the power of frequencies, especially on water, John thought that receiving a certain sound frequency would help our communications. So I downloaded an application on my phone, a frequency generator, and we meditate with the slight sound background of a frequency of 528 MHz. Why this frequency? It is supposed to, according to some specialised sites, regenerate our DNA. John feels this frequency well. Moreover, I checked my phone that I brought in the cave to emit this frequency, was is in airplane mode. I was able to check with a tester that no phone signal penetrates so deeply into the cave. Of the three frequencies he is talking about, is this one of them? And what is the third?...*
3. *John has this innate ability to feel the emotion generated by others. This is not really my case, even if I am beginning to understand why I feel more or less well in the presence of some people.*

Session 31 - 12/07/2022

In your conditioned world you measure everything in terms of size, big, small, in between. This does not exist. Another created illusion by you. Mass, you measure in mass, in volume. So, all the universes in the world would only create one grain of sand on all your beaches, and not even that. So it is also important for you to understand mass. Size, there is no size in the metaphysical world. It does not exist. You're a tiny, tiny particle in a universe full of infinite particles. This also collates with one moment, one time, no size, no mass, no volume. Your form can change anytime in the moment, and it changes all the time, constantly. Although you have created many forms, many forms are no forms. These are the things you will find it very difficult to understand because of your desire to have size and volume, mass.

The energy of a particle can disappear to a metaphysical form in a moment and reappear as a particle in another moment. This is what your scientists do not understand. They do not know where it goes because they do not study the metaphysical. Appear, disappear, of course it does not disappear, it is formed energy in the metaphysical. So, your conditioned logic will always apply itself to size, volume. You can be anywhere you like in the moment. You are.

You are correct to follow this path to understand more about the metaphysical world. You are correct that it is the only path you can choose, within what is occurring now in your world, that will allow you to understand what is occurring in your world. It is, of course, not the only path you can choose, but it is the correct path to choose. It will make more sense to you when you evaluate all of the different possibilities combined with the structure, a uniform structure. It is not by chance, it is not by accident that we communicate with you. It is by choice, by your choice, and by our choice.

Your conditioned life is insignificant to this journey. Your many conditioned lives are insignificant to this journey, insignificant in content of conditioning, not insignificant in knowing. There is a big difference between the two. As you become more aware, then you see the conditioning within others. You will awaken more. You will know more. You will experience much more.

I find it insignificant to talk to you about the specifics of the occurrence in your world today, but you seem to want me to go into detail. The detail is insignificant. The process is happening.

It can be changed in a moment; nevertheless, it is occurring. I tell you many times, it is of no concern of yours, but your conditioning will always draw you back to the detail. And, of course, you can learn many things from the detail, many scientific things, but there is no necessity for you to do this. The data already lies within, within you. But you keep going back. This is your conditioning. This is the piece that you hold onto, the piece you won't let go. But eventually you will. I tell you this many times: you will not let go. It is what you chose to do.

I think you have a clearer understanding now of the process. It is true to say that anything that comes from your imagination is correct, that transpires from your imagination is correct. Imagination is working with your subconscious, which will move into your consciousness, where you will be aware, you will know. You must try to develop your imagination. It is a very important part of the process.

You are constantly looking for comfort from others. But they may also be on the same journey as you, aware of the things that you are now aware of. But there are not so many as you think. And it will be impossible for you to explain your journey to these people. They will show an element of intrigue, but you do not have to search for these people that you are wanting to meet. They will come to you. This is the law of the process. They will come. They will come to you just as the two of you came together. It is the same process. And you would say it is the law of attraction. This is half right. There is much more to it than this. There is much more designed around this than you are aware of, but if you are happy to accept the terminology, the law of attraction, for you it is correct.

Your life here is evolving exactly as you planned it to. You may not think so sometimes, but it is exact. It is the exact that you chose. You must observe the circus, the carnival, the parade, the theatre. You must observe. You cannot interfere with this. You must watch, and you must learn, learn how the human race destroys itself, learn why it destroys itself through fear, learn how it destroys what it has created, how it chose to destroy what it has created. It chose; you chose this process for a specific reason. This is something we struggle to understand. We fully understand the process, but we do not know why, time and time again, you would repeat the exact same cycle. But within it we do believe there is wisdom, there is energy from the source. We do believe this exists within this process.

You must re-read and consume what is written, what is stated in the last two sessions. You must understand more the process. You are still missing something. Time, there is no time. The moment, there is only one moment. There is no time. There is only one time. There is no mass; there is no volume. You must re-read to understand more. You have a good understanding of self-created illusion; you have a good understanding of emotional frequencies, but you must learn more about the moment, about one time, one moment, one point that can change position. Position is important.

You are aware of many things now. You are aware how difficult communication is with your created language. You are aware of all these things now. You must dig deeper. You must be more patient. You would say, "Rome was not built in a day." You chose to create time. You must be more patient within it, within your time. It is only a moment. You must also engage in what you have created. Again, I tell you the same. Why would you create such a vast entity and not participate within it? Vast only in your mind. So you must engage, and you must be patient. There is much more to know. You cannot know unless you do know. You must also consume the energy within this space. It is good for your consciousness to experience this. It is clear.

Session 32 - 13/07/2022

So, you asked yourself a question, and you answered it. I have told you before: all the information is within; all the data you require is within. You can often do this: you can ask a question, and you can answer the question, because you already hold the information *(1)*. Your conditioning always tries to create a story. This is what you do. Why is it so important that you know the answer to these questions? It is your ego, you know this. Your ego will always create a story.

The origin has no beginning and it has no end. It is infinite. It is an infinite journey. You chose many cycles, many situations, many people. And you played these cycles through your choice. It was your journey. It is your journey of experience. There is no necessity to play a game in the cycle. There is no necessity to remember the detail. Your intrigue, of course, your ego, your mind will want to know the detail. Your origin is the source. This is where you come from. You are a pure form of energy as we are. It is the same thing, no beginning, no end, the source.

I can tell you that you have both taken many forms in your cycles, many. Male and female within the human form, and many forms outside of the human form, both. The details are irrelevant, insignificant. Not of this earth, you would say. But irrelevant, it is the same thing.

So, you asked the question, and you answered the question because the information is within. You are also correct to say that the now moment is the only thing that is important. And this is how you can make a change in your position. Very difficult, I know, because everything has already happened. Your past and your future, in what you call time, has already happened. But you can change in the moment. Difficult for you to understand, and you will never truly understand all whilst you are in the position you are in. But you will be able to see, to understand a part of this process. Fear will stop your journey. Awareness will allow you to continue. It is very simple. Fear is created by you, by your mind.

You are connected to all. There are no better or worse than you. They are all a source of energy. They are all on a journey, a journey of experience, of discovery. And, again, if you help them, you are helping yourself. If you know yourself, you will know them. It is an easy process to understand. It is not complicated.

So, things have changed again in your moment. The energy has changed again in your moment. You would say you are being attacked, but you are not. The energy has changed in your world that you created. It has to rebalance. It will rebalance. This is nature. It has no choice. This is the source. But it has changed; you can feel it. And, of course, in the world you have created you will witness many things. But it has little significance to your journey. Your journey is much bigger than this. It is much greater than this. Remember, you created it. How you would term good and bad is not. Them and us, it is not; it is the same thing. I tell you again: it is the same thing. They are you; you are them; we are you, from the source.

We find your choice of journey interesting. Your origin has never always been a human species. We find it interesting why you would choose to take this journey when you know, and you have always known. We find it interesting to know why you would take such a difficult journey. And we believe it's possible that we can learn from this, so we can help you also. We can help each other.

The two energies in this space, not us, but you two energies are completely different through choice. Through choice, and to meet. It is necessary to have a balance, to complement. Ultimately, the same energy, but on the journey, different. It is necessary for the journey, and has been over and over again, again, by choice. What an adventure you are having!

You must stop trying to apply your logic to every situation, your conditioned logic. It is impossible. It does not work. Of course, it works in your created illusion, but it is not real; it is not correct. You must use your imagination to create outside of this logic you keep applying all the time, your conditioned life. You must use your imagination to create. You can create what your logic will tell you are the craziest things, and they are not. Nothing exists you cannot create.

So many unknowns have been created in your world to leave your scientists completely at odds with their life. They do not understand. For decades, for centuries in what you call time, so many things have occurred. They cannot imagine why. This is imagination. This is creation through frequency. They have no answers because they use their logic. They use their conditioning to try and rationalise. It is impossible *(2)*. When they step outside of this, they can understand. Very few can understand; very few are able; very few chose the gifts you have to rationalise, the tools you use to rationalise, to imagine, to understand. You chose. You must keep searching. You must keep asking the questions. It is open. It is clear. You must know. You must know self. Know self and you will know all.

I do not consider any other species to be any different than us. They are all from the source. We do consider, however, that some know, and some do not know. They are different types of energy. Your energy is very strong, both of you. You cannot be manipulated. You will always be drawn to the source, always. You will be guided towards the source, always. This is why you have nothing to fear. This is why you are protected by the source. But, of course, your conditioned life will draw you back, as you chose it to do so. This is what you chose.

Notes:
1. *At home, John wanted to do an experiment about the fact that all the answers are inside each of us, and indeed, he received the requested information.*
2. *We often wonder about the conditioning of scientists, for whom imagination could almost be perceived as blasphemous…*

<u>Session 33 - 15/08/2022</u>

It is important to spend time, what you call time, within the world that you created. We are happy to see you join us again, even though we never left you *(1)*. There is much for you to learn. When you spend time in the world that you created, there are many distractions, many new illusions for you to create. But you need to know the answer to your questions, of which there are many questions and many answers.

Of course, there is no time. It is your illusion. There is no wrong; there is no right. Again, another illusion that you have created in your world to exist within it. So, how do we explain that to you? It's difficult. There is a uniformed pattern to all of this, and this is the key to your understanding of it. Even though it appears random, it is not. It is uniform. It is precise. It is from the source. It is one, one time, one moment where everything and all exists. This is the piece you have to understand to enable you to move forward.

There is at the moment in your world a stationary position, a mundane long process of nothing, no movement, no development, no thought. You also have to understand this: you judge it in time. It is not. It is a moment. Most are feeling the same, but for you this is unimportant; your journey is much different than theirs. Your journey is to understand the reason you exist, what you are, what you are made up of, which is pure energy from the source. The fundamental basics have been explained to you many times. No judgment, no hate, no good, no bad. You understand this in its entirety. But there is much more.

Based on this, there is no judgment for you to go out into the world, and do whatever you please to do, whether this is money or egotistical fame, fortune, pride. No judgement. But lessons will be learnt by you. You chose this path. You chose to make these decisions. Free will is what you have. Free will is your best attribute to enable you to experience, to enable you to grow, and understand what is happening around you now, to enable you to understand the process of the world, the change in the energy that is occurring now. This is based on free will. It's based on your own judgment of yourself. You might call it confidence. It is not confidence; it is awareness. You cannot hide from this. I know you don't want to hide from it. Most people are hiding from a decision that they need to make based on their own circumstances, their own situation. You are not hiding. You are seeking. You are seeking to understand. It is the correct way to go. Of course, correct is your words; there is no correct, but it is the way to go to enlighten yourself, to understand more about yourself, yourself being the most important person to understand. Self-awareness, most important. You chose this path.

We—I say we, as us, as you—we are never without you. We never left you. Left, there is nowhere to leave to go—it is your terminology. Once again, there is nowhere to go, to go to. It doesn't exist. You create whatever you want to create, to experience whatever you want to experience. There is nowhere to go, nowhere to leave to go to. You merely grow as an energy. You become more aware, more understanding of people and life. You experience more in your life to make you aware. You chose to do this. When you use words like leave and go, it is not possible; it does not exist.

And, of course, you are both a different type of energy, which helps you both to understand each other. If you did not understand each other, you would be the same. Both is necessary to understand one. Both is the same. It is one. It is one form of energy, of which there are eternal endless forms of energy, infinite forms of energy being created in what you call time, consistently in the moment. The moment is the real explanatory for time, the moment, one moment. Your imagination is key to understanding this.

Your access to information is endless. It's infinite. Your curiosity will want to know how this formed, where this came from. It is the same thing. It is one moment all at the same time. You have created so many stories. You have marketed—your words, marketed—these stories, so many brands. It is much simpler than that; it is much clearer than that. There is no necessity to do this. It is complex. But you like to create complex situations with much detail attached. For your journey, your imagination creates many complexities. It is for entertainment also, your ego's entertainment. It is a make-up of the energy that you consist of, is your ego. There is only love, love from the source.

So, you live two lives. You live the life you created here, and all the other lives you created before here. And you are now understanding the metaphysical world, which is actually the only life. There is only one life, but you live in both. You must see now how complex this is for you. It is not complex; for you it is complex. Your created imagination and thoughts to live in both, well, it's impossible. There is only one life—in the way you would term life—there is only one. There's a metaphysical life. But you have created another life to live in. You have created this world, and you have created these lives in this world to live in. So, you make it complicated. You deliberately make it complicated. This is something we do not understand.

I can explain all the science to you if you like, but it is unnecessary. Maybe for your ego it is necessary, but it is unnecessary to explain God's science, the source of the science. It is a process. It is a defined process. It is precise. It is perfect. But for you and your scientists it is random and complicated. It is not. It is of perfection. Yes, it always makes sense in here *(2)*, but of course, out there it is conflicting to the world you created, and it will be. But this is correct. This was your choice.

The girl you think about is also connected. She is also connected to the source *(3)*. You must help her. You must guide her. She is already guided by us. You must encourage her. There are very few, fewer than you think who can have access to such wisdom, not knowledge, wisdom. We all have access to knowledge, infinite knowledge, but wisdom is different. Wisdom is from the source, directly from the source.

Do not judge what you call the sheep *(4)*. Do not judge them. They are the same as you. They are on their journey, the same as you are on your journey of experience. They also created the world they live in. They chose like you chose. Do not judge. Do not be frustrated with them. Love them. Give them the love that they need. Raise their vibrational energy; raise it. They are in need of assistance; help them to raise their vibrational energy. Do not interfere with their life. Do not condemn them. Help them to raise their own energy levels. This is what you must do. You chose to do it. Do not fight with them; do not fight with yourself.

The channel is clear. It helps to feel sometimes human emotion. It helps to feel the pain, the love. You will stay with us.

Notes:

1. *After stopping for almost a month, John being on holiday and needing to step back for awhile from the sessions…*
2. *In the cave.*
3. *He's talking about Dawn, a close friend of John and Tina, very 'connected', but also entwined in her own difficulties.*
4. *I think he specifically addresses John, very often calling 'sheep' those who follow the rules without asking questions.*

Session 34 - 17/08/2022

Yes, it is always hard to know where to start, so many questions. We, too, so many questions for you from us, it is the same. We have told you many times we are close to the source. We do not understand fully the source as is the same with you. We know your species is closer to the source in many ways. And, yes, we do need to understand more. We search for the answers as you search for the answers. It is not a game as you perceive it to be a game. It is the search for wisdom derived from knowledge. Knowledge is infinite and is already within. So yes, we do need you in the same way as you need us, to teach each other.

You ask, are we Greys? This is funny. It is ludicrous. We are whatever we want to be whenever we want to be. Your interpretation is childish. It is like that of a child. I have told you before we are metaphysical. We are not physical, but we can take the form of physical if we wish. In an instant we can do this, and in an instant we can let go. So maybe we take the form of a Grey, maybe we take the form of a human species, maybe we take the form of whatever we wish to take, but it is irrelevant. The form is a machine; it is a vehicle. It is not real. It is not from the metaphysical world. It is a form. We can create any form we wish to create. We can create a new form if we wish to create it. So your question, "Are we Greys," can you see how stupid this question is to us? It has no relevance.

The Greys you talk about, your world talks about, your media talks about, they are a race, a race of what you would call ET that are controlling. They are a controlling race. They wish to control. They have a basic understanding of the process, but they have no understanding of the source. None. They live their life like a bee lives its life, in a hive. They work for all within their community with only a few working for themselves. Fundamentally, they are no different than you, than your species. They are the same; they are controlling. So your media is probably correct in their interpretation of the Grey, but this is not us.

Your ego has taken its place again with your question. Your mind, this is the difficulty that you have, the separation, the separation to be able to know yourself. I have told you many times it is very important to know self, to know yourself. If you know yourself, you will know; you will know all. Do you see the importance of the metaphysical against the physical world you have created? The physical world you have created is insignificant in the metaphysical world. It is only a theatrical story that you have created.

We are, or we consider ourselves to be, powerful in the metaphysical world. We are a pure form of created energy in a metaphysical form, so we do consider ourselves to be worthy of this. But you too are the same as are all the same. Realisation of this allows you to have the ability to do what you wish to do. You already do this without the knowledge, without knowing you are doing it. This is the difference. We know you know. We know you have done it many times. We know you choose to forget; you choose to have no memory. Every time you do it you choose to have no memory. This we don't understand; this makes no sense to us. This is why we need to understand why you do it, what is the reason you do it.

You talk about self-sacrifice to the source. We do not understand self-sacrifice. We are part of the source; what are we sacrificing? You must ask that question: what are YOU sacrificing to the source? What is the point? Yes, you are confused now, but it is a simple question. What are you sacrificing to the source with self-sacrificing? We do not know. We do not practice this. Why would we? It is very simple: if you become aware of all, there is no reason to do this; it is futile. The cycles you create are futile, but you create them over and over again. The complexities you create are immense within the world you live in, but you keep repeating the same cycle over and over again.

Of course, we can feel love for each other. We do feel love for each other. We feel love for each other, and we feel love for you. We are part of the same thing. There is no need to question our intention of love. We understand this philosophy very clearly, and always have done. It has no relevance with self-sacrificing. You say it is the source trying to understand the source. This is confusing to us. The source is all seeing and all knowing. Why would the source do this? But you seem to know. This is confusing.

We also know lots of things that you do not know, and we are happy to teach you many things. Of course, trust will always come into the equation from you. Your created world is reliant upon trust. Our world is not. You will always question everything. It is what you do as a human species; you question everything. You need to trust. It is necessary for you to trust. We do not. It is not necessary in our world to trust because we know. We understand why you question; it is your conditioning. You are at a crossroads. It is a bridge you need to cross.

You ask about the process; you ask about the uniform pattern. It is perfection. It is a perfect pattern. It is created by the source. I have tried to explain before how it works, but it is difficult to explain this to you. You have to use your imagination. You have to construct this yourself with your imagination, not with your mind. The pattern is very clear. It will come to you in an instant, in a moment. You have detail; I have given you detail. I have told you about the sphere. I have told you about things that will give you the direction to understand the uniformed pattern. But all I can tell you is that it is completely perfect; it is perfection. Unlike your thoughts of random, it is very precise. Of course, your imagination can make it random. Of course, you can go out in all tangents to create what you want to create. Confusion, deception, you can do all of these things. But it is all the same thing. It is one perfect moment for all. This is created by the source. We know this. The origin is the vibration of energy created for you by emotion. Of course, we feel emotion, but we manage it based on the process. You do not. You do not manage it. You are erratic with it. But the end result is the same. The process is perfect. You cannot change the process; you cannot alter the perfection of the process. Just because you behave erratically with your emotions does not mean that the process does not work. It is the same thing. It is another way of getting to a position. A position is more important than anything. These are the things you need to understand. You need to understand the process. I cannot make it clearer to you. There are no words; you have to feel it; you have to know it. You have to remove time; you have to remove mass; you have to remove volume.

It is true to say that your great scientists have worked with us, in the same way you are working with us now. But they are in your form. They, like you, cannot completely close the door. It is impossible. But they can have insights into the process.

When you doubt your experience within this area you are now at, it is only a moment. We know there is really no doubt. This is your conditioning once again. You are metaphysical like we are metaphysical. You have taken many forms like we have taken many forms. You have chosen every single one for a specific reason. It is not necessary to constantly feel emotion, to project that energy out onto others. It is not necessary. Therefore, you will learn—if you do not know already, which I think you do—you will learn how to control that emotion. To others this may appear harsh. It is not. It is precise. It is correct.

We have always been in control of our own destiny. We do not envisage that this will ever change. We do not perceive a time as you know time, that this will change. Why would it? We do not understand not being in control of our own destiny. We are not aware of how this works. It appears that you like not being in control of your own destiny. We do not understand why you would feel this way. This is interesting to us, knowing your history, knowing where you have been before, what you have done before, within what you call time—it is the moment. It is interesting to us why you would choose this path.

We can adapt ourselves to any type of human emotion, laughter, love, joy, pain. But we choose not to. We do not see the necessity to do this. We can, if we wish, do it. Sometimes, we do adopt compassion. Sometimes, we adopt compassion for all and every, but there is no necessity to continue this process over and over and over again, like you do. You believe it brings you closer to the source.

We are trying to help you to free yourself from the life you have chosen, to be aware of the reason you chose it, to understand more the metaphysical world, which is the only real world to exist within. We believe we are helping you, but we also believe that you may be able to help us to understand more the source. I know this is what you think, and it is correct.

There are other energies trying to communicate also. We live in a vastness of energies. There are as they exist in your world, a huge amount of different opinions, different positions, different energies, different times, dimensions, all in the same moment. This is a special place for communication. We do not stop them from attempting to communicate with you, but we can assure you that they are different than we are, in many ways. Yes, there are many.

Note:
In this session, The Man In The Cave answered all the questions we asked ourselves.

Session 35 - 23/08/2022

The question you ask is fundamentally simple. Why is the position you sit in a good place for communication *(1)*? You only have to know of your own experiences in life, where the energy is knowing to you, or it is not knowing. You can feel the different energies when you travel across what you have created. It is the same; it is the same for this place. It has a different energy. Energy, what is this? It is you. It is everything you have created. Different energy is more acute, or it is more subtle. It is more as you would say, powerful, or it is less in its appearance. So, this is the place where energy can come together. This enables a clearer communication.This is what you are experiencing now.

Your physics would explain a lot of this. But, again, it is a process, a simple process, a formation of frequencies that collide in a position that allow you to open the vertical. It allows you to correspond with, to communicate with a channel. You are a receiver and a transmitter of energy as we all are. And in certain positions and places, this energy is what you would call stronger. We would call focused; there is a difference.

There are indeed places of the same in the physical world that you created through matter, through frequencies. There are indeed other places where this occurrence is possible. But this place has a strong energy focus, a coming together. You would ask why this place? It is an accumulation of many things. Your own energy has a play in this, both of you, as does ours; it is the same. Your own choice has a focus in this. It is a process. It is a correct pattern of the formation of what you call matter. All elements have a play in this process. It is not the first time you have been in this area. It is not the only life you have visited this cave, for the same reason always, to communicate.

We prefer not to give names for places. They are insignificant to us. Many other energy forms will want to give you such information, precise information of their terminology, of their existence, of their creation. But it is the same thing. We do not have names, in the same way that you prefer to give everything a name. A name creates another illusion, another story which for us is incorrect. Of course, we know what you are referred to in this particular life you have chosen. Of course, we know what your names are. We prefer not to express your energy form in names. It has no significance. It feeds your ego. It feeds your human desire to be wanted, to be needed. We prefer not to feed this desire. This is the reason we do not use your language of names. Whilst you are still working within this world you have chosen, then we will do all we can to prevent you reverting back to your conditioning. Using names will only encourage you to remain in your conditioning. It is very simple. *(2)*

When you can accept that everything happens in one moment, when you know this is the case, you will be fully aware of all that is occurring at the exact same moment. The balance of energy in the world that you have created is volatile. It is up and down. It is volatile. It has to be rebalanced. It will be rebalanced. It is inevitable that it will be rebalanced. There is no escape from this —escape, there is nowhere to escape to. But this has no significance. I think you are aware now it has no significance in the real world, not your created illusion. The metaphysical world is the real world. And your awareness of this will prove. Do you need prove? Do you need to prove anymore your awareness? So long as you remain in the world you have created, you will always need to prove.

It is true that within the space you are now sitting in that you can create different types of energy. There are many things that you can do within this space if you desire to do so. We desire to communicate with you. You may desire something different. It is very possible here for you to create whatever you want to create, to do whatever you want to do *(3)*. You merely have to be aware of this. There is nothing to fear. But also be aware from us that it may shock you. It will surprise you. Once again, this is your conditioning, your inability, your inability to want to understand. You must know.

It is also true to say—yet again, more questions you ask—it is also true to say that from the creation of life in the world you have created that it is necessary to go through the whole process. The whole process is the creation of life within this world. So to become a form of the same as you, then we too would have to go through the process, the whole process. But we are also aware that the whole process has no time. So for us it is irrelevant *(4)*. You would measure the process in time. We would not. But we still have to go through the process, the same as you have gone through the process many times, because, after all, the process is the human form of life.

Reward is not measured in the metaphysical with any type of material gain. Reward is not measured in the way you would perceive reward to be measured. We would say that reward is awareness; it is wisdom; it is a closer relationship with the source. You would say reward is recognition; it is valued in material form. The only reward that we recognise is a reward from the source, of the understanding of love for all and every. This is the ultimate reward, as you would term reward. For us, the search for knowledge and wisdom stands at the highest point. There is nothing that we can be rewarded with that is greater than this.

Self-awareness is a part of this that allows you to know, to know what I am saying, what we are saying, what you are saying; it is the same. Everything in your life here, in this life of which you have had many lives in what you call time, lives that are continuing now in what you do not understand as time, many lives and experiences are building to the same position, a position of awareness, of knowing, self-awareness, self-knowing. You must experience all things to get to this position. You have chosen to do this.

There is not one thing that you cannot create. There is not one experience that you cannot experience. All and everything is available to you within a single moment. You must be aware of this. You are learning to leave behind your conditioned life within this particular life you have chosen. This is good. You are learning how insignificant what you once treasured, and thought was of most significance, is now only an illusion. This is good. And you are also learning that the repetitive cycle that you keep applying to your lives is not necessary. We too are learning from you. The position you are creating for yourself is the correct position, always. The path you are choosing is the correct path for you, always.

When you look into the darkness, you must look deeper. When your eyes are closed you must look much deeper, and the darkness will soon turn to light, and the light will become brighter and brighter and brighter, until eventually it is so bright you cannot look any longer into the light. This is the source. Your initial vision is darkness, and the darkness forms into a pure brilliant white light you can see. This is the illusion, the analogy of the illusion you created. The continuation of the creation of darkness, and your awareness of the light that lies beyond the darkness, is extreme. It is so extreme, it is so powerful you cannot even look at it for so long. This type of energy is formidable. There is nothing to fear to come deeper into the metaphysical, deeper into your consciousness. There is nothing to fear. You must travel as deep and as long as you can. You must remove all of your reservations. You will not lose anything. You will gain much. You must not hang onto your ego, to your conditioning. You must move into the light to experience, to gain wisdom. Yes, you have but a taste of the feeling *(5)*. This was your choice of journey, and you are experiencing all you chose. It is only emotion. It is a process. It is a release of energy. You must go back now.

Notes:
1. *This notion of position is important and delicate. Is it the geographical location, the cave, or also the state of consciousness, or both?*
2. *Clear explanation of why we feel a cold, clinical side in him, in addition to the explanations given in the previous session about their management of emotions and their adaptation to human emotions.*
3. *During my personal meditations in the cave this week, I tried, in vain, to bend a fork by thought. Probably my ego needed to prove something…*
4. *Answer to my question of whether they need to go through the birth process to physically manifest themselves to us.*
5. *John had an extremely intense visual experience during his trance.*

Session 36 - 28/08/2022

"Be of like a child to get through the gates of the Kingdom of Heaven" comes from your Christian teachings. And it is true. As a child you have little conditioning. As you grow older, you become very conditioned. It is the conditioning that you have to lose. It is a very simple statement of reality, one that is taught many times in your religions, and misunderstood and misinterpreted many times in your religions. A very simple statement: the removal of your conditioning will allow your awareness to develop the metaphysical—what is real, not what you have created within your illusion. The Kingdom of Heaven is the metaphysical world. It is the creation of the source, of what you call God—we call the source—which is a simple process. Not so simple when you lie within it, not so simple for you to adapt, nevertheless, a simple process.

It is also true that you do need to be aware of what you call time. There is only one moment. It is also true that you can change your position within this moment, within an instant. There are many variations of choice defined by your awareness, defined by you knowing. Your position will always be defined by your awareness. The insignificance about what you discuss, about what is happening in your world, applies as insignificant purely because it can change in a given moment. All and everything can change in a given moment. It is within your control how you change it, how you adapt yourself to it. Whether you hang onto it, whether you do not is your choice, because it is your illusion; it is your creation. This is why it is insignificant. It is your own imagination that has created it in the first place, and it will be your own imagination that will choose to not allow it to form, even though it has formed in a moment. This is something you need to understand how this is possible. How is it possible, you ask, if it has already formed, how is it possible that you can prevent it from forming? These are the questions you need to ask. It is about the position.

What lies in the metaphysical is truly a wondrous experience for all and every, truly beyond anything you can actually imagine at this point. And whatever you can imagine is whatever it can be. Again, defined by conditioning now, applied by your logic, which is incorrect. Your logic is the tool you use to create in the world you have created. Your logic does not apply in the metaphysical. When you use logic to work out a given situation in a physical world, it appears to be correct. It is not. Again, beliefs, systems you create, social, social acceptance, all of these things have a huge effect on your decision, on your conclusion.

We would consider ourselves to be a higher form of awareness. We do not consider ourselves to be above other entities and energies, but we do consider that we have a higher knowing. This does not make us in your terminology better or worse than any other energy or entity. You are with us, as you always have been. You are a part of us. You chose to go through this process again and again and again. You are at where you should be, precisely. It is not the same for all. You measure your progress, whilst you have communicated with us, you measure your progress in terms of your awareness in terms of time. This is not important. In terms of awareness, it is. You are becoming more aware, both of you, less concerned about what is occurring in your created illusion. This is correct.

There is nothing to do other than what you are doing now, to become self-aware, to focus on self. When you are self-aware you are completely aware. Know thyself; know thyself and you will know God, the source. I use the terminology God because it is the terminology that you always revert back to given your conditioning. It is the source. Know thyself, and you will know the source. And all is the same as you, as we are; it is one.

You desire always to have a higher, what you consider to be higher level of communication, of experience. This is what you are experiencing. Your wishes, your desires, you are now experiencing this. You chose to experience it, both of you. We too chose to experience this. From the position you are in at the moment, you subconsciously chose it. From the position we are in, we consciously chose it. There is a difference. We do not believe that we can give you any more knowledge than you already have. But we do believe we can make you aware of this, and it will awaken once again the wisdom that you already have, and it will allow you to be free from your conditioning once again. We do not know if you will choose again the same cycle. We do not think you will, but we do not know.

Your position is exact at this moment; it has not moved. Your energy is precise; it is exact. There is no reason for us to remind you to have no fear. You do not. Yes, it is way beyond your original expectation of what you could experience, and, of course, you can experience whatever you want to experience. You are slowly realising the insignificance of the world you have created here to what is the reality. But you choose. Wrong and right, there is no differential; they are the same. Whilst you are in your physical world, it is necessary for you to participate within it. Because every time you participate, you experience. Then you become more aware of what is occurring within your own self. No wrong, no right, participation is merely experience.

You must try to apply your imagination more. Your imagination is key to your development. Your imagination is one of the most powerful tools that your form of energy has. It is the origin of creation. The word has been misinterpreted for so long in your world. It has been undermined, underestimated. Your imagination is an incredibly powerful tool, one of the most powerful tools you have at your disposal. You must create with your imagination, and complete your creations with your imagination. You must visualise your creations; you must visualise your process, and you must complete your process using your imagination. Then you will create whatever you consciously choose to create, not subconsciously and erratically, but precisely. So you must develop and grow your imagination in every aspect, in every aspect of every relationship you have with everybody, in every aspect with your practical appliance in your life. You must use it at every given point you have. You must visualise, and create, and close, and repeat again the same process in every aspect. This is true creation, created from the source.

If you have fear of anything, then it is not correct for you. It is not correct for you to be controlled by fear. You must eliminate fear from your life to enable you to grow and become more aware. You must not allow yourself to have fear. I know this is difficult for you, because situations will arise within this illusion that will cause you to feel the emotion of fear. You must suppress the emotion of fear. It will prevent you from creating. It will prevent you from being aware. Fear comes from within self. You create your own fear; it is not created by the source, even though it is a part of the source. Whilst you feel the emotion of fear, the energy that fear creates, you will never be able to change your position. Your energy is highly formed so therefore, you can apply all the things we talk about.

You must not compare the love from the source by utilising your language of love. Your interpretation of love is not the love that comes from the source. It is very difficult for you, within the world you have created, to separate and understand what the love from the source really is. You must not compare them. Your love and the love from the source is completely different. The love from the source encompasses all and every type of energy that exists. It is the origin of all, all energy forms. Again, your logic, or your application of your physical logic will confuse you.

Go and enjoy what you have created. Experience what you have created. Know what you have created.

<u>Session 37 - 29/08/2022</u>

If you are an artist and you take a pallet of colours, and you mix two colours together, you get a different colour. But the colour you get is never the same. It has a different shade. And if you take at random the colour, you can never repeat the same colour you got in the first place. It will look the same to the human eye, but it is not. It is different. The particles you have joined are different. The shade is different. This is using only two colours. Imagine if you take all the colours on your pallet and you mix them together, and you create the shade of colour that you create, imagine how many different shades you can create by mixing the colours.

This is energy. Imagine the infinite amounts of strands, of colours and shades from all the emotions that are taking place in your world at the same moment. Imagine how many combinations of colours you can create. This is what you create constantly. You mix so many colours together. You never repeat the same colour. You always create a new colour. Whilst the old colour still exists—and the layers and layers and layers are endless—endless forms of energy you create, and these energies come together to create more energies, more emotions, more confusion.

You have to understand the basic fundamental of the original colours on the pallet without mixing them together. You have to understand the basic fundamental of those colours, of those simple energies. The confusion you create is unrecognisable from the origin of what it was created with. You have to understand the origin. You have to strip it back to understand the origin. You cannot consistently keep mixing the colours to be aware of the simplicity of the colours you originally started with. This is energy. This is the energy you create in the world you live in, the illusion you create with this energy in the world that you live in.

It is far simpler than that. You create these energies because you wish to create them. You chose to create them. You chose to create chaos. And now you choose to understand why you created chaos. And you are getting to the point where you will understand why you created chaos. We too want to understand why you create so much chaos within the world you have created.

When these energies are formed there is no going back. You form them with your imagination. You form them with your actions. You created them with your actions. And as I said before, there are certain points where energies come together. But the energies that come together are the original form of energy, not the confused form that you have created, but the original pallet of paints that you started with. This is where we are at now. This is the point where the original pallet is created, the point of imagination. This is where you sit right now with the original pallet of paints, with the ability to use your imagination to create your great and wonderful designs, or your chaos, whichever you choose. This is why it is a special place. This is why you are here, to understand this, to be aware of it. This is why the channel is clear. It is not contaminated. It is pure.

So in what you call time you can go forward with your creative pallet, but you can go forward knowing what you want to create. You can go forward with intent, with intention, knowing what you want to achieve in the world you live in. If you want to achieve anything, and you can achieve anything with your imagination, your imagination is the tool that puts all the pieces in place and allows them to be processed. Process must be followed, must be completed. This is done with your imagination.

You have a very charged imagination. Charged, what does this mean? You have a very formed imagination, a very trained imagination, and often a very volatile imagination. You must work on this.

Colours are important, and you get emotional energy from colours. In the illusion you have created, colours are very important. As too are sounds. They are all independent energies that collate into something else, born to develop into something else. You give them life with your imagination. This is why you are so drawn to music, the creation of a sound, an emotion. We too are drawn to colours and sound which evokes emotion, always. There is no finer form of creation than sound. Not words, words are different. Your words, your created words can confuse you. The meaning is all that is important, not the words. The emotion behind the words can confuse you when the incorrect word is used with the emotion. And you interpret the words in whatever way you wish, often incorrectly. But sounds are different as too are colours. Light evokes feeling always.

You must not ask, you must not ask such practical questions all the time. It is unnecessary. Your questions are born from your conditioning *(1)*. You must use your imagination. You must think outside of the box, your words. You must always think outside of what your perception of normality is, because often there lies the answer, not within your secluded conditioned world. So many people live in a box, and they see no way out, no door, no window, no light. You do not. So spread your wings, fly high, use your imagination to go wherever you want to go, whatever you want to create. Use your imagination because all and everything exists for you. There is no box. It does not exist. It is an illusion.

You have been with us for all of eternity, your infinite energy. You have worked with us for a very long time. You have stepped out of your comfort zone on many occasions; this we admire. But we don't understand; you have chosen to do this on many occasions. We know you never left—as we said before, there is nowhere to go—but we do wonder often why.

Yes, there is a lot of boxes being created now, a lot of prisons. You can see them like a mosaic of rectangles joined together. A prison, a prison for men. The individuals have created their own prison, and they are joining their prison with everybody else's prison. You can see (2). The circle, the sphere cannot join; it cannot join with another so easily. An atom, a molecule, it has no necessity to join; it is already one.

An army can be broken by one thought. A thought can spread like a virus through an army. It can be broken quickly. One simple sentence, one thought can destroy an empire. This is the power, the power of the source. This is the power that you all have with your imagination and your ability to adapt the process. Your mind will apply through the correct process with your imagination. Your mind is merely the tool. Your imagination is the command. You can create or you can destroy, you choose. There is no right or no wrong. But you must be aware; you must consciously be aware of this power, this energy.

We do not live in a physical form so therefore, in your world we have no physical position. We live in the metaphysical which, if you were to view it in the terms of your logic, it would be a space. You would not see anything other than a space. A vast empty space is how it would look to you. But it is not. The emptiness is full of vibrant incredible experiences and different dimensions. But you cannot see this. It is overlapping every empty space that you perceive is an empty space, that you believe is an empty space which, of course, it is not. It is where we live. It is our home. But we don't choose to randomly go to many different empty spaces as you would perceive them to be, which, of course, they are not. We have many people in contact with what you would call ET entities, different energies, who do live in the physical, who do have planets like your planet, which they live upon and travel out of. But we do not do this. I could not begin to explain to you what you would perceive is an empty space would look like, because even the words 'look like' has no relevance. You have lived here also many times in one moment.

What you can see is not from our world. What you can see now is from the physical world, vast, I know, physical creation of entities, energy formation, huge to you in mass, but in reality nothing other than an illusion *(3)*.

Opposing forces *(4)*.

You will be seen by many.

Notes:
1. *I take this for myself because I had prepared the following questions before the session, some of which are very practical: what are the other factors making the cave such a special place to communicate? I need to redo the joints of my shower: can I do it only with my imagination, without interrupting my current life? How do you learn from us? Through our emotions, by being aware of our emotions? Did we, with John, prepare this life with you, so that you could live it through us? We are supposed to live different lives in many different environments, have you ever experienced a human form, a terrestrial human form? If not, why? If so, why don't you remember it, knowing that as a metaphysical entity, you should remember all your experiences? Why did my attempt to bend a fork fail? In fact, we will have important answers in subsequent sessions...*
2. *John is visualising a mosaic of rectangles.*
3. *John is visualising a gigantic black triangular spacecraft, perhaps several kilometres long, which he is able to describe accurately. He feels it very close or arriving.*
4. *John is trying to bring his two hands closer but does not succeed. He feels like a metal bar stuck between the two palms of his hands that prevents them from getting closer.*

It is true to say that we are formed from the same consciousness. It is true to say that we have the same journey, and it also true to say that not every consciousness has the same journey, that is a journey of understanding, of knowing. We do not consider ourselves of a higher consciousness than that of you, but we do consider that we are aware of our consciousness, and we know that you chose not to be aware within the journey you are now making. This interests us. This is the reason why we communicate with you. This is the reason why we look down the ladder to find the reason why you chose, why you chose this route. You are from the same as us. Why would you repeat the lower self?—not lower in your interpretation of lower. Why would you want to be unaware, asleep, and go through a process, yet again ,of awareness? Why would you choose this journey? Why would you consciously choose this journey? Because you did consciously choose this journey. And I will repeat yet again, when we help you to awaken and become more aware, we are helping ourselves; this is universal law. Do you really want to awaken having chosen to come into this world asleep? It's a big question. Why would you want to go through the process again and again and again? Maybe there is something that you missed. We do not know. We also look to the higher self, the higher consciousness. We believe the highest of all consciousness is the source. We are not the source. We are part of the source as are you; as is all.

We only know of nine. We are not aware of twelve. This you are learning. You can call it levels if this suits your terminology. Nine is one; it is the same. We know there is higher than nine; we would call this the source. We are nine.

You cannot compare the metaphysical with the physical. I tell you this many times. It is impossible. You cannot apply your physical logic to the metaphysical world. It is impossible. You have to view things from a metaphysical view to understand the process, although the process is the source's technology. Do you think you can teach a new-born baby to fly a helicopter? Of course not. Bit by bit, piece by piece, you are becoming more aware. But there is so much more. In fact, there is so much more for all of us. It is infinite. You cannot comprehend the source, the energy. It is impossible for you to even imagine with your imagination what the source is.

When we talk about the love from the source, we talk about the word love because your interpretation of love is positive. Source energy is positive energy and negative; it is both. But your preferred word is positive. Positive and negative are the same. The word love to you encompasses the necessity to be wanted, to be needed, to be a part of. It is why we use the word love. Your insecurity in the physical world is drawn to the word love. It encompasses freedom, free will. It encompasses knowing. It encompasses light. Yes, you can see it now, light. It encompasses the creation of everything that is physical, and physical is what you believe you know. You do know some, but not all.

You are also correct about the translation of words. I have spoke many times about words and your confusion with translation. Your given confusion with the translation of words is so limited. We work in emotional frequency. We work in the light, the knowing. Words are so limited in expression and explanation, so limited. So as not to confuse, the channel has to be pure. I have told you why the channel is pure in here already. And it has to be pure, because otherwise the confusion would engulf you.

When we tell you there are nine levels, it is what we know. You have cause to believe there may be twelve levels. We can neither confirm nor deny this because we do not know. We only act on knowing. This is what we know. We are a world of metaphysical, and this is what we know. You are from the level of nine. It was your origin. Your birth of energy came from the level of nine. Your birth was from the level of nine, and yet you choose to go back to one. We only remind you of what you already know; it is simple. And when we remind you, you know again; instantly you know. Whilst you are existing on the physical level of one, then you will often deny such knowledge.

Your interpretation of time, it is still difficult for you to understand time. You have a small grasp of this, but you do not know. You need to know. Remove all aspects of physical creation, mass, volume, remove them all, and you are left with what really is time: one moment, one time which we are all existing within the universe we are in, of which there are many universes, many creations, vast, infinite. So remove the physical element that prevents you from understanding one moment, then you will understand one moment. So long as you exist in the form you exist in, in the physical world, you will never understand one moment. It does not mean you have to leave your physical created world. It merely means you can experience all and everything on every level of consciousness as we do. You choose. You never leave. I have said before, there is nowhere to go. This is another illusion that you created: I leave and I go to somewhere else. How can you go anywhere as a metaphysical form? There is no mass, volume, material. One moment.

This energy that you can feel, a pure form of energy, a clear channel; you can feel it now.

We do not wish to tell you what your future is. It is irrelevant. It has already happened. We are not as you would term fortune tellers. There is no necessity for this. If only you could realise how child-like this question is. The only thing that is necessary is to understand. By knowing yourself, you will understand, because you are us. Your insignificant human life and your desire to be needed and wanted is also a process that you have put yourself in a position to endure. It is also irrelevant. No, it is not just irrelevant to us, it is also irrelevant to you. You just do not realise how irrelevant it is.

Yes, you are teachers, like we are teachers *(1)*. We do not interfere as you do not interfere. But we evoke reaction through conscious thought, which evokes growth, growth for the energy that you all are. This is what you do. This is what you have chosen to do.

You can feel the force, the power now. Again, this is pure energy *(2)*.

Your journey, as is the same for our journey, will lead you back to the source. And your choice will be to make another journey, or to reside within the one. It will always be your choice. It is a sphere of which there are many positions, and you choose which position you want to reside within. There is nothing to fear within any position that you reside within. There is nothing to fear. You chose for a specific reason. To experience, to become aware and awake is the reason you chose. Every consciousness is not the same. Neither are they below you. In their form of energy, they are the same; in their position they are not. It is completely different.

You cannot, you cannot force energy. It flows naturally. You are resisting the energy. It is impossible. You must allow it to flow. You created it to flow. You like to challenge *(3)*. Acceptance will bring wisdom. Challenge creates the journey to find it.

By the laws of attraction, people, consciousness, will be drawn to you of the same as you will be drawn to them of the same. Once again, a part of your creation, your desire, your knowing, your choosing.

Harmonisation of particles is necessary also for you in the physical to create pure form of energy that exists. It is not contaminated in here. It is good that you continue your journey of discovery.

There is no necessity in your life for gimmicks. You are way above that *(4)*.

Notes:
1. *Of course, being a teacher makes sense for me, given my professional career as a sports instructor And in the industrial environment in which I also worked, I constantly wanted to transmit.*
2. *For John in trance.*
3. *For John in trance, trying to control this energy with his hands. But it can also be what happens when we try to interfere in the life of those around us who do not share the same journey as us...*

4. Obviously, this is our little fork bending experience! Explanation: for several sessions that The Man In The Cave asks us to participate, create, in physicality, and use this energy available here in this cave, I have decided to conduct a simple experiment: to bend a fork with my mind. I took this fork several times to the cave during my personal meditations, and nothing happened... until tonight! When we left the cave at the end of this session, we find with amazement, in a great burst of laughter, that the fork, left on the table of my terrace, it has indeed bent!

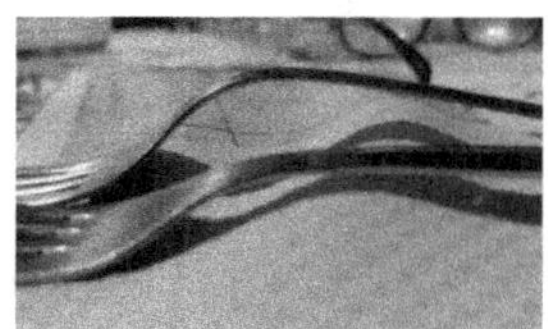

I therefore decided to go further and tried to reproduce this phenomenon on another scale, as well as to ask this first bent fork to bend more, by demanding a 90 degree torsion angle, in order to show my total control over matter! But during the following days, nothing happened... except that on two occasions a few days apart, my gaze was attracted by a strange phenomenon: the shadow of the fork that I had left on the table and moved several times, had created the 90 degree angle requested!

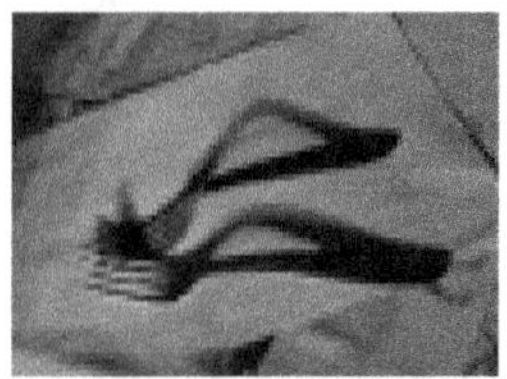 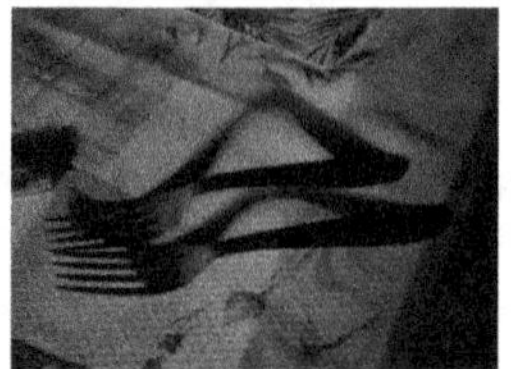

Session 39 - 11/09/2022

The law of attraction is a mirror reflection of self. You will always be attracted to entities or people that are relevant to the position you are in at the time—in what you call time—you are in. You may also be attracted to certain entities, certain people that you think you should not be attracted to. This will create change in your life. There is a specific reason why you chose to be attracted to these people or entities before you start your journey. This will confuse you, knowing that these entities or people are not the same as you. But there is a specific reason you choose them. But the law of attraction, like attracts like, is for a different reason. Your journey is a journey of discovery, of enlightenment, of awareness. So therefore, people will be attracted to you of the same. It is a journey of experience.

You wish to know more about the different dimensions. They are one. They are the same principle as the separation that you individually apply upon your world. Separation of people is the same principle as the separation of dimensions. You can be born from the beginning, from the origin into any of these dimensions. You can be born from the beginning of your origin into all of these dimensions. You have been in all of these dimensions. You chose to be in this one. An understanding, an awareness, an awakening is knowing all, not knowing only one, of which they are the same. We know of nine. We communicate with you from nine. You live in a physical dimension; we live in a metaphysical dimension. One is not greater than nine, neither is nine greater than one. Your interpretation of greater is incorrect. They are the same. They are the same in value. They are different in experience.

It is true to say that our interpretation of life, of consciousness, is very different to your interpretation of consciousness. That is what you chose to come into this life with knowing. Does not mean you are not subconsciously aware of all, because you are. It is not the same for everyone or every living thing or every consciousness, of which everything is consciousness. Many in nine have not been in one; many in one have not been in nine — been, it is the same. You have been in all. You have experienced all. In what you call time is irrelevant, it is in one moment. You have access to all in one moment. We are not aware of ten, eleven or twelve. Six is metaphysical, six to nine is metaphysical. One to five is physical. Four and five have a greater understanding of the process. You as we, are a part of the source. We, like you, are also learning.

The law of attraction will define, it will define your energy and your direction. It will allow you to be free, free from isolation, or what your perception of isolation is. There is no isolation. You are not alone. You are one. It is merely your perception of isolation, your fear of isolation, chosen in the physical world you live in, chosen deliberately to expand your awareness. One to nine are not separate. They are not isolated from each other. They exist as one, together. And within this space you are able to communicate with all. Again, this is your choice, and so it is our choice. But the dimensions are very different which, of course, makes communication difficult on the basis of language. True language is frequency, vibration. It is not spoken, not spoken with the word as you have developed, but the pure energy that is used, created by the source. It is clear communication. It is not contaminated. It is pure energy. This is what you are experiencing now. You have learnt a lot. We too have learnt. Again I say to you, by helping you we are helping ourselves. But it is the same thing; we are you, energy from the source, so we might as well say we are helping ourselves, as one.

The source is expanding, but it is a cycle of expansion and delivery back to the source, a constant cycle. So it is both: it is both expanding, and it is both understanding of one, a circle, a cycle, a sphere.

Position is most important. Time is irrelevant as is mass, volume. When I say irrelevant, I am not talking about your physical world being irrelevant. I am talking about irrelevant in the vast consciousness of all. You must not apply your physical logic to the vast consciousness of all of the dimensions. There is no rationale to do this. It confuses you; I must say less and less, but it does confuse you. Your physical world is very relevant, but also very small if you interpret in size, which we do not. From the start of our communication with you, we have also learnt many things. If you do not know, you must seek out; you must find out. There are no secrets. There is only experience. Your desire to know exceeds everything as does ours. It is the same.

The complexities you created, in this physical world that you live in, have entrapped people on a vast scale of energy. But this is no concern of yours. It does not affect you. It does not affect your awareness, or your growth, or your development. It will correct itself. There is a vast change occurring now within your physical world, but it is insignificant within what you would call the big picture, the whole of consciousness. There are physical entities that are, you would say, fighting for supremacy within this game they are playing. But, again, it has no concern of you. It is no concern for you. It is a small piece of an infinite jigsaw of consciousness which is ever evolving and expanding. And in the moment, it can change. Its position can change. You create that change.

You see now how insignificant the questions are that you asked at the beginning of this journey. You can see now how they have no reflection upon what truly is what you consider to be life or consciousness. It is a wondrous feeling for you to now be aware that these things that you believed were significant are totally insignificant. There is much for you to learn, and there is much also for us to learn. You could say we are so far apart, but we are not. We are so close. We are the same. I did tell you how insignificant your questions were, and I think you now understand why. Your journeys are the same as our journey: to become aware, each and every, of everything. And you must also experience the physical world you have chosen to belong to. You must also continue to experience all and everything that this word has to offer you, a world that you created. It is the same as the world that we created, that we all created, from the source.

You can also see now how all of the basis of the basic religions are formed. The story is the same. The basis is always the same. But it is childlike. It is only half of the story.

No more gimmicks. It is not necessary for you *(1)*. You must relax and accept what you know. It is not necessary to prove anymore. It is only necessary for you now to enjoy your journey, to take pleasure from your journey, to enlighten others to join you in your journey, to experience all and everything, physically and metaphysically. It is no longer for you to have to prove anything. There is no necessity to prove anything. You are aware; you are consciously aware. You must develop now the skills that you know you have. You must develop yourself.

You have come a long way, and there is an infinite way to travel. Truly an incredible journey.

Note:
1. *Probably an allusion to our fork bending experience...*

Session 40 - 15/09/2022

For me to explain space and time in the words that you use, more importantly the words that you understand, is very difficult for me to do. Your scientists, your greatest scientists have been working on this for decades. They themselves with their knowledge of mathematics and physics, they themselves do not know. It is a knowing within. You have the information already within you. You must seek out that information. You must know. It is one moment. Time as you interpret time, you created time in the physical dimension that you have evolved yourself in. You created this time. It is not what time really is. There is only one moment for all experiences of all consciousness, one moment, one point, one position, which can change in that moment. There is no travel, no distance, no mass, no volume. It is difficult for me in your simple words to explain this, and it is incorrect for you to try and understand this in terms of physics and mathematics, because they do not understand it; let alone, you, to understand it this way, would be impossible. We co-exist in this moment, in the space where you believe nothing exists. You think it is an empty space. It is not.

We are co-existing within a different dimension within this space, in the moment, as so are you, as so is all consciousness existing within one moment within this space. What you have created that is physical is what your senses tell you is real. Of course it is not. It is your illusion, your created illusion. The emptiness of, or what you perceive to be the emptiness, is where all exists in one space, in one time, in one moment. Hence, nowhere to go because we are already here. Energy, frequencies collide and form different frequencies and different energies within this space. Communicating is a part of this process. Jumping from one dimension to another is a part of this process. Understanding the value of this is a part of your process. You must dig deeper for the answer; it lies within. Knowing this will free your mind, your conditioned mind. Knowing this will open up to you many possibilities, not in the way you would term them, not in a practical way, your given physical practical way, but in an infinite eternal way of knowing. Basic theory of understanding this, you have little grasp of.

A crossover of the dimensions can be seen in your world many times. Apparitions, you would call them ghosts. They are not. It is a time warp as you would term it, but it is not. There is no warp. It is happening in the moment. It is being created in the moment. Your terminology of prediction, you are not predicting anything. You are merely observing what is occurring. It is the same. But it can change in the moment. You have the ability to change it with your imagination.

You are correct when you talk about theory and practicality. We do not experience the practicality of your physical creation. We choose not to. There is no necessity for us to do this. But we do observe your emotional reaction to the practical world you have created. It is of great interest to us, certainly considering that you understand subconsciously all aspects of all dimensions.

You must travel out of your physical world, out of body, to understand time. To know what one moment truly is you must travel—travel, of course, is the word you would use. This is likely to be the only way you will understand time, dimensional time, and energy. So it's difficult for me to explain this to you in the limited vocabulary you have created. Words, it is not words, it is energy; it is a feeling, a frequency, a vibration. This is the only way you will understand this.

It is also true to say that as you are becoming more aware, we are watching your experience. We are monitoring your experience. We are learning from your experience. An awakening is truly a magnificent experience. You chose this journey, and we have great interest in it. We are all created from the source, source energy, the origin of all dimensions, the origin of all created metaphysical and physical consciousness. We need to understand better the source as do you. We can live your practical experience, your physical experience through you, because you are us. We can smell and hear and see and feel through you, because you are us. It is the same thing, the same energy. It is literally only one word. Experience is the reason you chose to journey, to experience, to become aware. It is no more complicated than this. There is no higher or lower as you term reason. There is nothing more for you to do other than experience, to know yourself. Know self.

Your egos, your created egos have created many reasons why you should do this, you should do that. It is unnecessary. Know thyself, and you will know the source. Simple. There is only one, and that one is the source. And you are created by the source so therefore, you are one. How more simple do you want to hear it to be? And yet you make it so complicated with your ego, your ambition, your fears, your wishes. There is only one because one is the source. One is everything, is all. Separation is discovery of knowing self. Separation is understanding and knowing self. The cycle is the same in every dimension, the cycle of knowing, becoming aware and back to the source, to the beginning, and start again the cycle, in one moment.

It is by no chance that you make this journey. It is by no chance that you chose this journey, and it is by no chance that when you become more aware, you feel an incredible enlightened experience full of joy. None of it is by chance. It is your choice as it is our choice. I keep saying to you your words are so limited; they are so limited.

You choose not to communicate with lower dimensional entities. It is not our choice; it is your choice. We would not prevent this. We understand why you choose not to do this. There is no necessity. We do not know of ten, eleven or twelve. We believe there are only nine. So to go higher, we cannot explain to you higher—of course, higher, your interpretation of words, there is no higher or lower—but you choose not to talk to what your interpretation of lower is, lower dimensions. You have done in this life, historically, communicated with such, but the channel in here is pure; it is clear. There are many that do sit with lower dimensions; many do communicate. Also, many in your physical world are in communication with what you perceive are lower dimensions. Dark and light are from the source; it is the same energy. You do not fear this as we do not fear anything. You see little necessity to communicate on anything other than the level you are at, and, of course, there is no necessity to do this. Your experiences by now show you this.

Stay in the positive light. Both negative and positive, plus and minus, are correct. But you must stay in the positive light. This is what is good for you. This is your journey. A journey of awareness is creativity, and positive, for the moment you are in.

Session 41 - 19/09/2022

It is better to feel than it is to think. The vibrational energy of feeling is far more effective than the thoughts from your mind. It is your imagination. The answer to your question about physics, your great scientists are better to use their imagination to get the answers they require *(1)*. Their answers do not lie within their calculations. So you can help them much more than they can help you, because on their journey they are not helping themselves. They are relying on your physical knowledge of science, not of their awareness and feeling, not what the answer is. The answer lies within them already, but they do not access this. You do. A feeling, a knowing, not in your world, a science, is two completely different concepts. So it is true to say that they need you much more than you need them, if the right word need exists. A better word is experience, teaching. Their own illusion, their own journey in their own mind will put them on a higher pedestal than you, much higher within their own illusion. If they can achieve both—when in reality the only one that is important is awareness—but if they can achieve both, then they will understand. But they will not understand any more than you will understand because the information already lies within them. They will understand in the same way that you will understand. It is not a difficult process. And it is true to say that some do understand. And it is true to say that some do understand, but deny the inner wisdom, the inner voice that talks to them. They deny for fear of condemnation, for fear of ridicule within the system they have created. The complexities they have created with their own imagination, their own minds, having trapped them. They have stopped their progress. They have built a wall. If only they knew how simple it was to remove that wall or not even to build it in the first place. So, it is a fact that you will be able to help them more than they can help you. And their complexities, you have no necessity to get involved with. It will only confuse you. But it is two different languages, two different worlds of understanding, but the same, the same conclusion. Your intrigue has brought you to this point, the point of knowing, the point of understanding as all will follow their intrigue, as all do follow their intrigue to discover and experience. But not all lie in the same position so therefore, the connection is weak. The connection with these people is weak. It is a very small candle burning.

You do not have to be concerned about your attraction to certain entities and beings. They will be attracted to you as we are, as we are one. It is a uniformed pattern of attraction of frequency, of energy, which is natural, a natural process that cannot be diverted. Your ego requires you to force this. It is not real; it is your ego. It will happen naturally, just as with everything will happen naturally as a course. There is no reason to be worried or concerned that it is not going to happen. It is happening already to you. It is a course, a flow, a natural process. Why would you worry? Why would you be concerned? You work too hard on this. What do I have to do? You don't have to do anything other than what you are doing: to become more aware. Step-by-step process, you would say written in stone, immovable, absolute, without doubt.

You see little point in creating more experiences other than the one you are having now. This is not good; it is not bad. It is what you are. But you mustn't be afraid of creating experiences other than this in the physical world you live in. It is all one big experience. Your awareness will not diminish *(2)*.

What you are looking for you will experience soon. We cannot, we cannot guide you into this. It is your own doing. Your own energy will find its course as it always has done. Energy formulates and disperses as do clouds in the sky. It is a similar process. Formulation and dispersion, a constant process, particles forming and dispersing with all the energies that your physical world is constantly putting out. The frequency, the vibration it is a constant forming and dispersing, and appears to be chaotic. It is not chaotic. It is formed; it is dispersed; it is recreated; it is constant. Your mind construes this as chaos. You believe it to be chaos. It is not. It is uniformed. It is creation of physical matter.

You have the ability to own all of the senses, not the few you have been designated with and chosen to have, all the senses to see and hear and smell and touch this, of which there are many in the physical world, many, many senses working on a metaphysical basis. It is not a question of the metaphysical meeting with the physical. They exist in the same time and space. They are one. You chose to separate them. It is a question of understanding this and allowing them to be what they are, one form of energy, one form of energy in one moment, all that is physical, all that is metaphysical, separated by your mind deliberately, deliberately and intended for you to become aware of this, consciously aware. The physicist's desire to know the answer to the questions will, ultimately, lead him to the same point as you. It cannot go any other way. It is impossible.

It is very basic, your experiences with people, very basic understanding of consciousness. For you it is intriguing, but it is normal. The cycles, the cycles that they continue their lives with, they are seeking position. They have position. Position can change in one moment. Not all is in the exact same position, but it is within one moment, and all is everything, one consciousness, one source.

Two elements, complex and simple. The same thing. You like to involve yourself in the complex. The more complex it becomes, the less you will understand it. It is simple. There is no necessity for you to make it complex. That is your ego, your mind.

Notes:
1. *We question ourselves, John in particular, about some great 'connected' scientists such as Tesla or Einstein, who received information as soon as they used their imagination rather than their intellect. We also wonder about scientists with no spiritual approach and the impasse they are in.*
2. *For several months, John and I have been reluctant to resume a lucrative activity, especially for fear of collusion and incompatibility with our spiritual journey. On several occasions, The Man In The Cave encouraged us to participate more in this world that we have co-created.*

Session 42 - 21/09/2022

Your energy in this world is of a physical nature. You have physical senses. You chose this. Your conditioning often prevents you understanding the metaphysical world of consciousness. Due to your senses and your physical being, you often apply the same logic to the metaphysical. This is incorrect. It is like talking different languages. One is one language; the other is a different language. You have to learn how to separate the metaphysical from the physical, and then you have to learn how to talk the language of the metaphysical, of which there is no language, no words: it is vibrational energy; it is emotional; it is frequency. This is where your confusion lies: you cannot apply the logic of the physical world to the energy of the metaphysical world; two different worlds completely. When I say to you, you have to think in terms of vibrational energy, it is difficult for you to do this. I know you have done it all of your physical life, but it is difficult to only think and always think in vibrational energy, and never to apply your words. Your words will confuse you through your logic and understanding of words, which again is limited. The process is simple; you would say like riding a bike. The first time you have done it you will never forget. It is the same principle. And in the same way you apply that logic from the physical to the metaphysical is the same way you apply the same logic, not just in language but in understanding of process, understanding of time, understanding of the formula.

No mass, no volume, no time, but within both the physical and the metaphysical exists the formulation of atoms, of particles. Everything is made up of atoms. All energy is made up of atoms and particles, sub-atoms and particles. Sound, vibration, frequency is all made of atoms, so atoms exist in the metaphysical as well as the physical. Atoms are created from source, from the source. Atoms are the machine used by the source to create all consciousness of which there is only one consciousness: the source.

Atoms fluctuate. They appear and they disappear. This is physical form to metaphysical form, and back to physical form to metaphysical form, and so forth. This is the behaviour pattern of atoms. And, of course, your scientists do not believe it is possible for them to disappear. But of course, they do not disappear. They merely change their position. But because your physical world cannot recognise where they have gone to, they believe they are disappearing. They are not disappearing. They are merely becoming metaphysical, metaphysical to physical to metaphysical. They are being created. They are being formed. And this is done through your vibrational energy, your frequency, your imagination, your creativity. This is why they can appear in any position or point within your physical world, and, you would say, thousands of miles apart to reappear. But it is not. It is in one point, one moment. There is no distance to measure; there is no time to measure. Volume and mass can be dispersed easily to your perception of what is nothing. It is, of course, not nothing. It is a different form of energy as we are, as you are.

Energy will form in mass. There is also a uniformed pattern to the formulation of energy, of particles, of frequency. It will join together in mass through thought, through emotion, but it will always rebalance, plus and minus, to create a balance. But it will go through a process of forming in mass. By this, I mean an imbalance. But there is a reason for this, a defined reason. You might like to say a machine will rebalance itself. It will. You might like to say that nature will rebalance itself. It will. It cannot possibly do any other. And, of course, with your erratic creation of frequencies and thoughts without the knowledge of what you are creating, it is necessary to rebalance the energy. But this is of little concern to you. You are already aware of this.

Your journey is different. Your journey is not to rebalance. Your journey is to live in a positive creation of energy, a positive creation of frequency of emotion, of light, not of dark. One is the same as the other. Difficult for you. One becomes the other. Difficult for you to understand. They are the same. Separation is by your choice. There is no isolation for any form of creation from the source. It does not exist. Vibrational energy of fear separates. The vibrational energy of the love from the source joins. But both are necessary for understanding and becoming aware. The only way you can understand is to experience because each and every experience will bring you closer to the source. And we also learn through your experience, through your emotional journey, often confusion.

There is only one consciousness. We do not know what lies after this. We do not believe anything lies after the source. It is a constant cycle, generating energy and changing energy. And because you are a part, you are also the whole. You are a part of the whole so therefore, you are the whole as are we, the same.

It is very important that you consciously, now especially, consciously make your own decision. It is very important that although we can see many things that you cannot, within one moment, it is very important that we do not influence your journey or your road. It is very important that it is from your own conclusion, your own decision that you create your awareness. This is particularly important for the position you are now in.

You do not have to look outside. All the answers you require you already have. You have the same ability as we have to see them. The questions you have asked exceed most others within the world you are in. That's why there is no necessity for what you would call prediction. Gimmicks. It is much higher than that. There is no prediction. It is choice. You create it. You created it. Awareness of such will make you realise how ridiculous prediction is, the word prediction.

It is also true to say that your created earth has its own consciousness, as an entity, as a living machine, as does all created planets and suns and solar systems. It is the same in the physical, created consciousness working in the same way as you are, back to the source. Everything has a consciousness. Everything is a consciousness. Your word soul is very limited in the way you perceive it.

You are understanding more now of time, but you are not there yet. You must become purely metaphysical to understand this, to know it, to feel it. And although you meet with us here in a level of consciousness that is agreeable to both, a frequency, this is not the metaphysical pure frequency. It is decided from you and us the position where we meet. It is both energies' mutual ground. But the metaphysical is much different than this. This is where you will experience time and space. And you will; you have.

You must ask yourself why you feel so at peace with yourself within this area. You must ask yourself why nothing else seems to matter within the area you now sit. This is not an illusion. This is an example, a very small part of what exists within the metaphysical world. It is not fully metaphysical; it is a joining together of physical and metaphysical. If you feel this way here, you must use your imagination to feel what it will be like in a pure world of metaphysical. I could not possibly explain this to you.

I have told you many times the process is uniformed; it is correct; it is precise. You must take note that due to your conditioning you will apply many things within the process, branding, naming, badges. You will always want to do this. You are joined with a different energy today *(1)*. There is a need always through your conditioning to apply branding, badges, stories, names. There is none. It is a pure form of energy. The process is defined. The outcome is your choice. The branding and the names from your conditioning will confuse you. It will confuse your journey. It will inhibit you. It is created from your ego, from your fear, from your obsession to own, to label. This does not exist. It is your illusion, your fear. You are correct to say it is pure energy that we deal with in every level, so you must dismiss names and brands and systems that you create. This will inhibit your growth.

Consciousness is one pure form of energy. It has no block. It has no stop. It does not create a blockage for itself. This is you that does this within your conditioned world, your conditioned self. There is no good, there is no bad, there is only positive and negative form of energy. Both are necessary for your growth, for your enlightenment, your awareness. If you create a brand, this is where you will live. If you create a story, this is where you will live. You must raise your vibration above this to understand what you term physics, energy, vibration, frequency. You must raise above any type of story that is created from man, from yourself, from your conditioning.

The energy that has joined us today has many past lives, many experiences that she is subconsciously aware of. You are driven by intrigue as you all are. Your intrigue will take you to a place of more understanding, more understanding of the process, the dynamics. Words like God and Soul inhibit your growth, create a story, a brand. It is marketed by yourself. It gives you a false sense of security. God is the source, the source of all energy. The process is the process. It is not complicated. You make it complicated yourself. The childlike suggestions to you, given to you through your religious beliefs will inhibit your growth. You have to expand your consciousness to understand what lies beyond this. The ignition is there. The will is there. But you have to ask questions. You do not. You should not lie content with what you believe.

Your journeys are very similar. It is the law of attraction that created this moment. It is the law of attraction that will propel, always. You are at the beginning of a very exciting journey. There is much more to learn, to experience, to participate. It is only yourself that will stop your growth. You will constantly revert back to your conditioning for security, for the fear of growth. There is nothing to fear. There is only awareness. There is only the love from the source which is not how you interpret love. You must work in the positive. You must grow self in the positive. You must be self-aware. Know thyself. If you know yourself, you will know, because it is the same.

You must not hang onto ritual conditioned by yourself *(2)*. This is not a case of believing; this is a case of knowing. Knowing is more important than anything. When you know, there is no return from this; it is not a story. You must raise always your frequency, your vibrational energy, your positive energy. This is your journey. This is not the same journey for all, not in this moment that you are in. You must remember there are no coincidences. Nothing happens without a reason. Coincidence was invented by your ego. Your ego is necessary on the physical world that you live. It has a function. Your ego forces change within self, forces experience, and from experience you grow; you become more aware. You must never think you know; you must know. When you reach the point of knowing, there is no reason to question anymore. This is your free will. This is your freedom. This is the true interpretation of free will.

You must look within for your answer. You must not allow your mind to give you the answer *(3)*. You must know the feeling inside when it is real. You must feel this. This is true vibrational energy from the source. This is what you are looking for. This is what we are all looking for. There is a huge distinction between knowing and thinking you know. The feeling from knowing is absolute. This is the energy from the source.

There is no need to fear. Fear is a necessary energy created in the physical world by you. It is necessary again to propel you forward to awareness, a process that you go through, a process of fear and then awareness. It is your created process. There is no fear. It is not real; it is an illusion. You must remove fear completely. All energy is created from the source. Fear is a necessary vibrational energy that you adapt to the physical world that you are in. It is a tool.

The energy in here is pure. You must look more into the metaphysical to understand more how it works. Defined process, it is uniformed; it is correct. You should be here today.

Notes:
1. *For the first time, we welcomed someone to the cave to meditate with us. Isabelle, a friend of a very old friend wanted to participate. We had agreed with John, before inviting anyone, to ask them to read the previous sessions in order to validate their true interest. One person changed her mind, not feeling ready to receive such material. But with the volume now exceeding a hundred pages, it seems difficult to ask volunteers to read this amount of material. On the other hand, we require the reading of at least two or three sessions in advance. This is what Isabelle did, who was always ready at the end. It turns out that this session was largely devoted to her, even if, once again, these lessons are within general scope. This experience is also interesting for John and me. We are satisfied with this session and the effect we have seen on Isabelle. It seems to us that we helped without interfering, in an extremely direct and effective way. But of course, it is her choice now to continue her journey.*
2. *I think this is a remark about the protection prayer that Isabelle made before entering the cave. In a previous session, he had already said that in fact we pray to ourselves when we pray...*
3. *Isabelle has indeed cut herself off a lot from her emotions for years, and passed almost all of her decisions through the filter of her mind, her mental...*

I say to you many times what is occurring in your world in this time, in your interpretation of time, is of no significance to you. It has no effect on your journey, on your infinite journey. This is for you. It is not for all; your journeys are different. You have a different reason, a different position within your journey. It is insignificant for you. Your intrigue allows you to monitor what is occurring, and often this confuses you. This is the difference between conditioning and consciousness, awareness. There is no necessity for you to monitor what is occurring. You must stay in the positive, in the light, and continue your understanding of consciousness, your awareness. This cannot touch you. It is small and insignificant within the infinite world of the source. Your conditioning will always draw you back to what is occurring in the physical world that you live in, that you chose to live in. Your journey is infinite; it is endless; it is without time and space. This is the reality of life. Your illusion entraps you within it through your conditioning. You revert back always to your conditioning, your ego, your mind. This is the process that you go through. But for you it is insignificant what is occurring. It is a mass of energy created through vibrations. Joined, it grows. It will disperse; it will correct itself, but it is not important for you to be divulged within it. Your view on life should exceed and surpass this now, and understand the eternal life and journey that you are participating in. The acceleration of the negativity that is created in your world at this time, in what you call time, is phenomenal. It is explosive. It is created through negative energy. It is necessary. But, again, no concern of you. It will rebalance. It will reset. This is part of the process. It is not wrong; it is part of the process.

Many, many energies you are associated with, many people will be drawn into this negative void. You will feel pain from this. Your pain is an illusion. Your pain comes from your conditioning. You must lift your energy above this. You must work always in the positive. You chose to do this, and you must apply it. You will not be drawn into it. This is your journey. You chose to be here in this time, in what you call time. You chose this journey. It is not pain; it is awareness; it is wisdom; it is knowledge through wisdom. The love from the source encompasses all. It is not your interpretation, your physical interpretation of love; this is conditioning. You are connected to all. It is love for all. Your families chose to be around you at this time, in what you call time, for a reason. Although you don't think so, they did. They, like you, chose to be here and now, within the moment you call time. You are becoming much more aware of this now. There is no point to disagree, to argue, to fight; you are adding to the vibrational energy of negativity. It is pointless. You are not helping the situation when you do this. You must stay in the positive. Again, this is not for all. You chose this. You chose; you chose it. It is difficult for you to understand when you live in the physical and not in the metaphysical. If you apply always positive energy you will lift, you will lift your families. You may not think so, but you will. It is a vibrational energy. It can do no other than lift into positive. It is impossible for it not to work. It is the fundamental basic principle of the process. It is absolute.

The attraction of negative energy to negative energy is the law of attraction. It is happening en masse. Most cannot control this. They do not even know. They are not aware of what they are doing. It has taken you a long time, in what you call time, to understand this fundamental process, and you do now understand, and this is what you must apply. There is nothing for you to do other than remain positive, lift the vibrational energy through the frequency of emotion. Know what you are doing. You understand the principle, but you must know when you do it, when you apply it, that it is correct. You must feel that it is correct. Against all condemnation from all around you, you must apply. This is your chosen battle, your chosen route. Now you understand there is no right or wrong. And it is necessary.

There are many positions that a consciousness chooses to be in. This is why there is such a variation of stages of the process, but they all happen in one moment. No time, no space, no mass, everything is consciousness. But it is one, the source. We do not know beyond the source. The source is all creation, and you are a part of that creation. You must not indulge in negativity. You will be presented with many negative situations. You must see the positive within them, and rise above and create positive energy. This is what you chose to do. Difficult, I know, when you revert back to you own conditioning, but it is absolutely necessary that this is the course you take. You must not judge these people, these energies; you must not lay judgment on them. For them too, it is necessary that they go through this process. But for them it is a different process that they chose than the one you chose.

Your conditioning will initiate within you fear. You must overcome fear. You must rise above fear. Once you have done this, then you can apply positive energy. You cannot apply positive energy whilst you are in a condition of fear. You must accept and understand the emotion, the frequency of fear. You must know what it is. Once you are aware of what it is, it has no longer any value for you. It will be dispersed from you.

You are now beginning to understand what your journey is about within this time, what you call time. It is a marvellous experience for you. In what you call time, you have waited a very long time for this moment. You must participate within it in a positive way, a creative way, and continue to create positive energy. You are here; you are in the physical. You must participate in a positive way, directing always positive energy. You know what you must do, and how you must apply yourself. You feel the scales are tipped against you. They are not. Raise the vibrational energy in your physical world. Raise the positive vibrational energy. This is not about your ego. You did not choose a battle you could not win, which is your ego. You chose to be a part of something very special. It is not a battle; the formation of consciousness is not about a battle. It is not about winning and losing; it is about creation, experience, journey; no wrong, no right, experience.

Yes, wise words I am giving you. Now you must go and play your part.

<u>Session 45 - 03/10/2022</u>

Whilst you are consciously aware in a physical form, you will find it incredibly difficult to feel the frequency and the emotion of a metaphysical world. The only time you can achieve this whist in a physical form is to achieve what you call an out of body experience. Even within the process of an out of body experience, your conscious will still apply a metaphysical philosophy in that you will want to create a physical form within an out of body experience. This is not how we create. This is because you are still attached to your conditioning within the experience you are having in the out of body experience. So the complexities of understanding are immense. This is why it is important for you when you experience this journey to remove your conditioning completely, then you will truly experience the metaphysical. But this is difficult for you because you are thinking in a different language. This is where you will understand time, where you will understand mass and volume and space. You are constantly applying your conditioning to try and rationalise and understand the metaphysical. Whilst you will get an insight into this, you will never truly comprehend what metaphysical really is.

All energy is formed through frequency. All emotions are frequency. Formation of energy is vast; it is infinite; it is continuing, ever expanding. Everything is energy formation in the physical world. It is a very complex web of energy. There is no necessity in the metaphysical world for the continuation, the formation of energy in the way you are continually forming energy in the physical world. It is true to say that the energy is continually changing within your physical world. When I say it is insignificant, it is insignificant. You have to use your imagination to know what the metaphysical world is capable of doing, of creating. Everything is consciousness, every physical creation, a cycle of creation, changing energy from one form to another, a solid form to what you would perceive is not a solid form.

It is not a game. It may appear as a game to you, but it is not. All created from the source, a cycle, created, deconstructed, created, deconstructed, formed into different energy, recycled into different energy. You do not lose your identity. It is an egotistical thought that you would do this. You gain much. You lose nothing. You can choose: you can have one identity, or you can be a part of all, the source. It is one. You cannot comprehend this; this is your conditioning. The vastness of the metaphysical, the creation from the source is infinite, all-encompassing, overpowers everything you believe to be real in the illusion that you have created—it is a minuscule part of the process. You merely have to experience this, to know it, to be aware of it. This is your journey. You have what we would call a small understanding of it. You are at the beginning.

It is true to say that other forms of life within the source, the universe as you might call it, physical forms of life would like to intervene within your world. But it is difficult. It is as difficult for them as it is for you to accept that this is possible, because if they interfere with your journey, there is consequences for them. They can only inform. They cannot interfere. They will create energy that is not necessary for them to do. It is dangerous for them, for their journey.

I told you many times your journeys are different than most. You must work on removing all fear from your life of any kind, and think in the positive, always. Fear is a necessary tool within the physical. But not for you. You have chosen a different path. You must think, once again, in simplicity. Although you are capable of many complex thought scenarios—you are capable of dealing with many in one moment—you must think in simplicity, the simplistic form of energy, of creation from the source. It is now, in what you call time, your time to do this and to apply positive energy.

The vibration of your physical world will be raised. It will be corrected. The necessary cycle it is enduring at this moment will form into positive vibrational energy. The process is taking place now. Although there is only one moment, you must hold two places: you must hold a place in the physical, and you must hold a place in the metaphysical, and you must bring them together to understand the process of what is occurring. You have the capability of doing this.

You understand now how every energy in your physical world has created their own individual. Each one and every is an individual story, a brand around their own position. Whilst they are one, they have intentionally isolated themselves, each and every, only to form back to one, to the source. This process is occurring in what you call time, in the moment, now. As you would say, keep one foot in each space. It is a balance, a balance of the physical energy that you create. This is not new to you. You have a complete understanding of it. It is written within you, and you are remembering it.

There is nothing that happens that is a coincidence. There is a uniformed pattern to all of this. It is created by the source. Each and every person is an independent energy, an independent flowing energy, unique within self, within themselves; however, part of the source, as one. You will encounter these people in your life that have significance upon your journey also.

It is infinite. Infinity is difficult for you to understand. No beginning, no end, one moment. It is only position that is important to you.

Session 46 - 06/10/2022

You are energy. Your consciousness is energy. Energy is another word for You, for your being. This is why you are correct to say that positive and negative are the same thing. Formation of energy comes in many forms, formed through frequency, through emotion. And, of course, when you use words like negative, your conditioning will tell you that it is bad, it is not good. It is the same thing. It is a single form of energy encompassing all forms of energy, all creation. Again, your words deceive you through your conditioning. The formation of different energies under the whole of the source is infinite. It is ever expanding, ever growing. Your current understanding of this, although it is primitive, it is correct. So you must think, you must imagine when you consider energy formation, not in terms of positive and negative but in terms of one energy, one energy that can be an infinite amount of energies, just like you, just like the way you have formed yourself. It is the same thing. You are one of an infinite amount, but still only one, the same. Positive and negative is the same thing. It evolves into the same thing. It forms; it goes in a cycle of creation, and back to the source, as one. You are self-creators of energy. You paint many elaborate pictures with your energy, your formations. To experience your journeys, you do this. It is necessary for you to do this. But the formation is the same. It will revert back to the source, back to one. And it is uniformed; it is precise. You are but energy; it is what you are. It is simplistic, but many complexities created by you within it to journey back to the source, to the one.

There is nothing for you to do other than experience this process and be aware of it. You can help others also, to inform them only, not to interfere with their process, their position. The law of attraction will bring these people to you. The law of attraction merely adapts a procedure, a process. You too will be attracted to like, the same, the same type of energy you have created. But you must not allow your conditioning to confuse you, because it will. And you must not keep asking why, why am I here at this time, in this situation *(1)*? It will be a natural occurrence for you. It is true to say that many will ask the question why, and in what you call time, very soon they will ask the question why. But this is their journey. You have asked the question, and your question is being answered. And some will never ask the question. It is not their position. It is not their time, not in what you call time, but their time, in what time really is.

You cannot imagine the world of the metaphysical, but there is nothing to fear. Fear is an illusion. It does not exist in the pure metaphysical world. It is, again, your creation. The word on its own needs no other words to be associated with it to entice your mind into a different type of energy. And the word love you have adapted; you have grown insights, a different type of emotion, a different frequency. But it is still not correct; it is still not the love from the source. A word, well, we have no words to describe this to you that will fit in your vocabulary of words. It doesn't exist.

Yes, it's the same thing in a different way, a different way based on your position, a different way for you to understand what we are saying to you *(2)*. It is becoming much clearer to you, but there is so much more. There is so much more that you already know within. There is so much more that you can release from within, through awareness. But your basic understanding of the metaphysical, of the source, will guide you through this process. It is guiding you through this process.

You have been mixing chemical compounds for years in what you call time. This is the same process, the coming together of different energy to create a different energy of the two compounds that you mix. This is the physical formation of the metaphysical creation. The original form of energy can be pure as is gold is pure, a pure form of energy. This is your man attraction. Your physical attraction to gold is because it is a pure form of energy of physical creation. Whilst you are not fully aware of the attraction, this is the attraction. It is in a pure state of physical energy.

When you think about healing, you talk about the healing powers of crystals. For example, crystals emit a pure form of energy, and you receive that energy within yourself because it is pure; it is simple. It is healing. But it is healing on an emotional and energy level of frequency. This is why it works. Your emotions create the healing process of the physical because it is a simple and original form of energy, a pure form of energy. It is not complex to understand. But in your conditioned world, it is difficult for you to apply this. You have forgotten with your conditioning what these basic fundamental pure forms of energy are capable of doing in your life. You block them through conditioning. You do not allow the energy to take the process that it needs to take within yourself due to your conditioning. Your illnesses are created by yourself due to your conditioning, due to what you believe to be correct, when in fact it is only your illusion. There are many forms of healing that can be adapted to your physical being, but you deny them based on your conditioning.

You need to cross that bridge. The bridge exists. You must find it and you must cross it. You must cross it from your mind to your imagination where you will find this pure form of energy, the same form of energy that exists within the place you are now sitting. It is pure; it is simple. It is not contaminated with many, many types of crazy energies that you create. It is only necessary for you to understand this process. You may not apply the process always, but it is only necessary for you to be aware that it exists. If you apply certain parts of the process like the healing process, then it will enhance your physical well-being. But your physical well-being, your machine, is but a machine that carries your consciousness through. There is no point to be obsessed with the machine. It is the metaphysical that is important, not the machine. So it is necessary for you to understand this process. You are not going to apply this process of healing through desperation. You are beyond that within your thought process, whereas many will and many do, for fear of the end of this life. This process, they apply through fear. You are not going to apply through fear. You may apply through intrigue but not through fear. It is not necessary for you to do that. You are a machine upon a machine created by the source, the beginning and the end, and the beginning again, and the cycle of creation, not in space and time.

Whilst it is necessary for you to experience the physical world that you have put yourself within, it is not necessary for you to constantly question every day—in what you call time—your motives. There are no motives. It's simple: experience. Your ego will tell you, you have a function to perform. You do. It is to experience all and every type of emotional frequency, every type of energy. To exist within the physical is to experience the physical. To exist within the metaphysical is to experience the metaphysical. You are now existing in both. Many never experience both in the same position, the same moment. One foot in and one foot out is the way you would say it. Not everyone has a cave!

Do not try so hard to see energy in your physical world. Relax; you will see the formation of energy; you will see it. You have seen it before, and you will see it again (3). You will physically, in your physical world, with your eyes, you will see it. We have no necessity for eyes or ears or nose in the metaphysical, but you will see the formation of energy in your physical world.

Notes:
1. *We asked ourselves this question again just before the session.*
2. *He told us several times that he would repeat things differently until we understand.*
3. *We think he is referring to the auras that John saw but has not seen for years.*

Session 47 - 12/10/2022

Chaos and dysfunctional. You gave away your free will. You subjected yourself without free will. This was your experience *(1)*. You were not in control of yourself. This is the reason why you experienced this in this way. You did not choose. You allowed yourself to be led. By who, by what, would be your question. You volunteered yourself to be subject to no particular process. You volunteered chaos without awareness, without knowing, without being aware of what you are. Voluntary chaos is what you experienced.

I have told you many times that you cannot comprehend the metaphysical unless you are aware of what it is. Your awareness will happen; it will happen. It has happened within one moment. You cannot experience time and space within a physical form. You cannot use the senses that you have created for yourself in the physical world to experience this; it is impossible. Piece by piece, like a jigsaw, you will put it together. This is awareness. This is the process. Why would you want to volunteer for chaos? Your journey is to experience, to become more aware. It is a step-by-step process. This is the only logical, physically logical solution to embark upon the process. But, of course, physical logic does not apply in the metaphysical. But physical logic is the vehicle you will use to understand it because these are the senses that you have. Does not mean you will understand it with your physical logic. It means you will use your physical logic to create the journey to understand it, to embark on the journey. You have no other senses. How can you use senses you do not have? It is impossible. You cannot place yourself in a metaphysical world with only your physical senses.

The complexities that you create in your physical world will confuse you, but awareness is about all; it is about everything, all-encompassing, everything from the source. I have told you many times there is a uniformed pattern that exists within all of this.

The journey you cannot imagine. You do not understand the infinite journey in one moment. Everything encompasses one. There are not so many making this journey, but one is all. Again, difficult for me to explain to you. It only takes one to be all. Separation is by choice. Reality is one. So if there is one making the journey as all are making the journey, it is the same thing. There is no right way or no wrong way to do this. There is no right or wrong, no good, no bad. These are your words from your created illusion. It does not exist. There is only energy, and energy formation is vast; it is infinite, but it is still only one. Your created complexity in your physical form creates so many different forms of energy diluted from one form, the original, the source, and it is a necessary process to create all forms of energy that will eventually find their way back to the source. You must not think that the metaphysical world is separate from your physical world. It is the same. It is, in as you would determine a place, it is in the same place. There is only one place. Your words are limited again.

There is no wasted energy. There is no waste. Another word from your physical creation, waste, it does not exist. There is only energy created for a reason, formed for a reason, changed into a different form of energy for a reason, a uniformed pattern, a reason, a reason to know yourself, know thyself, be aware of what you really are. Expand your imagination; expand your mind. Cross the bridges you need to cross. Have no fear; fear is your created illusion. There is nothing to fear.

Whilst you are here in the world you have chosen to be, the physical world, enjoy; enjoy the physical attributes that you have created. There is no guilt. It is another illusion that you have created, guilt. It will slow you down as so does fear slow you down. All aspects of your creation are to be enjoyed by you in the positive. Remove the clouds that you allow to hang over your head. It is a wonderful experience for you. Piece by piece you are building, you are building your picture. Each part of the jigsaw you place, you become aware of the picture, the full part. This has all been created by the source. The source is infinite, and you are a part of that creation, and you have created your own illusion. Enjoy what you have created. It is wondrous. We too have created our illusion. We too enjoy what we have created, but it is much different than what you have created. You created time to allow continuation of the cycle; to stop and to start again was the reason you created time. It was precise, a precise creation to endure the process. This is your time. It is not metaphysical; it does not exist within the metaphysical. You used your imagination to create time to endure the process, the cycle. You can use your imagination to create anything and everything that you wish to create.

Your physical dimension, your physical world is the most pure form of created energy from the source. Although it is diluted by individual creation, it is pure, the first stage of physical creation. It is special. It is natural. Nature, it is attractive to other forms of creation because of its natural creation from the source.

It is important that you do not judge yourself. It is equally as important that you do not judge others. Knowing thyself is the ability not to judge yourself. As knowing others as knowing thyself, you will know others, and you will not judge them either. Part of knowing. Observation is different than judgement, but observation within your conditioning can bring about judgement. It is the—for you it is the wrong energy to use, not for all, but for you it is—the wrong energy to use to make judgement on anything, anything. Difficult, I know, but necessary for your awareness.

Where darkness meets light, you must stay in the light. This is where you must be. But remember, neither is incorrect. .

Note:
1. *Two days ago, John decided to conduct an experiment. In order to better understand time, more precisely the notion of 'one moment', the unique moment in which everything happens, and perhaps also to put both feet in this 9th dimension, he sought to put himself in a modified state of consciousness by smoking marijuana. The reason he chose to smoke marijuana was a decision based on an experience he had with marijuana many years previously. We immediately left to meditate in the cave. But the experience proved to be very negative. A nauseating physical sensation was added to a complete non-understanding of the experience, extremely unpleasant. He had to ask for help from The Man In The Cave, which he got, to get out of this state. The recording of this session did not work, but we knew that we would have comments during the next session. Here they are.*

Session 48 - 15/10/2022

It is important to try and understand the meaning of one, one moment, one time, one moment, one existence. We co-exist with you in one moment, all and everything in one moment. You will never truly know this until you are in the metaphysical, but you can understand some of this. One moment is time. All and everything in the same moment. One, this is one. You have separated yourselves on the physical, but you are still only one. Whilst your illusion convinces you that you are separate, you are not. You are not separate. You are all connected in one moment as one as are we all; it is the same thing. So, you use your physical logic to try and understand how this works. You will not be able to understand this with your physical logic and your physical senses. This is impossible to apply, but you will get a feeling of how this works.

We are here with you always. We never left because there is nowhere to go, as so are all the dimensions in one place, one time. You might say they are layered over each other. This is not perfectly correct, but it is the only way I can explain it to you. Knowing is being totally aware of this. You will never be totally aware of this in a physical form.

In here the energy is pure, it is clear. Out there it is contaminated with all the energies that are being created from each and every one of you. Contaminated is the only word that I can think of to explain to you. But contaminated is not bad. Your words have created many words that insight into you a frequency, an emotion of bad. You would consider the word contaminated bad. It is not bad. But it is the only word I can use to explain to you that you can relate to. It is diluted, the energy is diluted. It is complex. In here it is pure, it is clear. This is why we can communicate with you in here. It is clearer for you to understand. Out there it is not, because of the contamination of the production of many energies, infinite, constantly, in one moment.

Your physical human form is drawn to pure energy. You are all drawn to pure energy. This is the reason why you are drawn to grass, the country, the clear sky, and not the city, not what you have created, but what has been created by you from the source. You will always be drawn to clear pure energy and creation. It allows you to have peace. It prevents the speed that you can create within the world you have created, the speed that you can create contaminated energy, confusing for you in your conditioned world. This is why you are drawn to pure, natural, to nature, to the source. This is simplicity. Simplicity will bring awareness. Complexity will confuse you. And the more complexity you create, the more you want to create, through fear. You believe you have to keep creating the complex world that you live in, but you don't.

Your technologies are not necessary for you to understand consciousness, to understand the source. It is far simpler than that. Your technologies will take you further away from the source. Whilst they are fascinating to you, they will take you to a different kind of energy. They are not bad, neither are they good. They are energy created by you, your creations coming from the source, all one, and you must experience all and everything to become aware of this, to understand it.

You would say, again words, you would say it is your job to form a better relationship with God, with the source. This is correct, but not in the way you think. You were never without. You are a part of. You are knowing more; you are experiencing more the source, the creation, your creation. Your words, again I tell you, are so limited; they create emotional frequencies; they create energy which is incorrect because of the way you interpret that energy, the way you receive it. It is incorrect. It is very difficult for us to use language, the language you have created to allow you to understand. It is very difficult. It is far easier to feel. A feeling is knowing. It is instant. It is without question.

It is a cycle for each and every within the physical. You have created time to continue the cycle. It is how you measure the distance between the cycle. You use your created time. You create the beginning; you create the end. Another illusion. It is a cycle within a cycle. What you have created is from the source. You create many of your own cycles within the cycle. There is only one cycle, but you have created many, and you try to rationalise this with time. Your imagination has created many things through your given senses.

To know what others are thinking, you merely need to know yourself because it is the same thing. You will sit for many hours trying to work out what others are thinking. You do not need to do this. You only need to know yourself, then you will know. You will know exactly what they are thinking, how they feel. You cannot possibly know what others are thinking until you know yourself. Regardless of all the complexities that they have created, they are you. They are the same thing as are we. This is why you cannot lay judgement on them. You are laying judgement upon yourself. It is like a mirror reflection of you. If you initiate pain upon them, you are initiating pain upon yourself. If you help them, you are helping yourself. They are you. Know thyself. It is very simple. That is for all. That is for everybody. There is no differential between them. It may appear to you that they are different; they are not. Within, they are the same. Your illusions, your creations in your physical world will tell you that they are different. They are not different than you; they are the same. This is how you harmonise energy. This is how you create harmony, another word. It's difficult for me to explain without this word. Know yourself, then you will know, then you can apply.

With your eyes, your physical senses, formation of energy appears to you as though clouds form. You can see it. This is how it appears to you.

Session 49 - 17/10/2022

There is a big difference between what you perceive to be reality as to what reality actually is. Your perception is your confusion. Your judgment of others is your judgment of yourself. We have a different energy in here today, a confused energy, unable to separate her conditioned life from what is real *(1)*. Conditioning comes from the mind. It does not come from the consciousness, in your words, from the soul. Many past lives of conditioning create much confusion. It is very difficult to separate from these lives to come to the reality of consciousness. There are many reasons for this. You chose this path; you chose this journey. You do not think you would choose such a journey, but you did. You chose all of the people that you associate with. You must learn to understand yourself, because they are one, the same as you, one consciousness. By understanding yourself, you will understand them. It is a very simple process when spoken; it is a very difficult process for you to understand within the conditioned world that you live in. Your perception of problems are not problems. It is a form of energy to project you to a different position, a different point. It is not a lesson; it is an experience. There is no necessity for you to learn anything. The knowledge already lies within you. It is only your ego, your mind that confuses you.

Your perception of wrong and right is not correct. Again, it is only your perception, your life. You must remember, every single one of you has lived and is living many different lives in conscious awareness. This can be confusing for you within the one life you are focusing on. There is no problem other than within yourself. Your expectations of the people around you exceed the reality of what consciousness is. This is where you will find peace.

You need to understand that everything, everything in the physical reality that you have created is made up of particles, including you. Outside of this, there exists also a metaphysical which is also made up of particles through frequency, through emotion. You must understand that you are a part of one. You are a part of everything. Whatever you throw out in frequency and emotion will be received by all.

You cannot judge. You are only judging yourself. You are a part. This is all created from the source, what you would call God. There is no right; there is no wrong. It is experience. You chose to experience this many times. You chose to come back again, and you chose to experience it again without the memory of the vast consciousness from which you come. So to understand others, you must understand yourself; you must know yourself. You think you know yourself, but you do not. You cannot, you cannot lay judgement. This is where confusion lies. Confusion comes from your mind. It did not cross the bridge to the vastness of consciousness. You created your own confusion. You allow it to develop. You nurture it; you live in it; you enjoy it, even though you think you don't. The law of attraction will continue to create; to create, the more it receives, the more it will create. This is energy, frequency derived through what you would call your emotions.

There is no right way or wrong way; there is only energy. All and everything is made from energy. All consciousness is energy. Your interpretation of consciousness would be God, the source. There is no beginning; there is no end; This is your creation. It is correct for the physical world you chose to live in. It is correct. It is correct for you to experience the journey you have chosen. There cannot exist one without the other, positive, negative. Energy, every form in your physical world is made up of energy. It is made up of particles. You are made of particles. Your thoughts are made of particles. This is all created from the source.

You have created your own prison with your mind. You must know within yourself what you are, a pure form of energy as all are the same. By knowing yourself, you will know them because you are the same. You must look within for your answers. Strength is the ability to know thyself, and to see thyself within others. Once you can achieve this, you will no longer lay judgement; you will no longer lay blame; you will no longer point from within outside because within is all.

It is no concern of yours what is happening in the physical world that you have created. It is insignificant within the whole of the consciousness, the whole of the energy. You must be positive. But you must know; you must not think you know; you must know. There is a big difference between thinking you know and knowing. There is a uniformed pattern to this. You may not think so, but there is, there is a defined pattern, a perfect pattern.

I do not use names. Your human form likes to build pictures and stories around brands and names. You are energy. You are part of the whole of consciousness. I do not encourage you to create stories around this. It is these stories that you create that entrap you within. Your only job, if that is the word you wish to use, your only mission in life is to experience and to become aware of the process, to become aware of energy and consciousness, to become aware how this is formed. It is a process. It is only a process. It is for you to experience this process; you chose to experience it.

Do not fear. The energy of fear is what stops you creating. Do not fear anything; there is nothing to fear. Your life is eternal; it is infinite. Your fear will restrain you; it will imprison you. You choose to fear; your mind chooses to fear; your ego chooses to fear. Do not fear. There is nothing to be frightened of. It is a beautiful journey you have chosen.

Note:

1. For the second time, we are welcoming someone to the cave. This is Sandra, one of our neighbours. She also did not read all the previous transmissions, or even one, but her insistence on participating led us to invite her to the session of the day. Once again, in our opinion, the transmission was almost entirely dedicated to her even if, obviously, these lessons remain within the universal scope. After all, we are all one…

Session 50 - 20/10/2022

So much information, you are correct to try to understand it. But you will never be fully aware of it until you are fully immersed within the metaphysical. But it is correct to be aware of it. It is already within you, the full understanding of it in a theoretical way. To understand it in a practical way, you will need to be immersed within the metaphysical completely.

We are you; we are the same as you. You may use the word higher, higher self. This is not technically correct with the words that you create, but you are content to use the word higher. We are not higher. We are you. We are the same. You are also correct to use the word sessions. We are not teaching you anything. You are not learning anything. You are experiencing. It is an experience. So by applying your knowledge of a circle, a cycle—it is the same thing—you are correct. A sphere, this is what it is. But you cannot experience this in a conditioned physical form. Neither can you amass the information you need to have to understand it, to feel it, more importantly to feel it. But a basic—and it is very basic—understanding of this allows you to continue your journey. Without having this basic understanding, you cannot continue your journey within the physical world that you live.

You now understand how your physical mind, your ego, wishes to create a story around everything. And your understanding of the physical world you live in makes you create many stories around everything that you become aware of. It is important not to create these stories, not to give them names or brands. This will only confuse you. It will entrap you.

It is true to say that you have total free will to choose, to choose any given position within the sphere. Any position you like you can choose, but your position will only be given based on your awareness. And your conditioning will prevent you being able to choose certain positions, when in reality you are already in all positions in one moment. Difficult for you to understand this, but to understand all positions within one moment is for the metaphysical, in complete metaphysical.

You have chosen a very difficult path. It is frustrating to you, I know, but this was your choice. We do not wish to experience the same cycles that you have experienced, although we are the same as you. We separate ourselves from these cycles, and we watch you. We learn from your experience within these cycles you choose.

It is necessary for us to advise, but only advise on process, on application. We cannot choose your direction. This would not be advice on application and process, this would be manipulation. By doing this, we will harm ourselves. By helping you to understand, we will help ourselves. You have an infinite amount of choices. You can choose many or all, or one. It has all taken place. It is a ridiculous statement to make, it has all taken place, but this is how you understand it. It is all happening in one moment. There is no past; there is no future; there is all in one moment, one time. Again, difficult for you to understand this. It is all metaphysical with many created physical illusions within the process, created by many forms of energy in many dimensions in one moment. You are not just living in this moment, but within this moment you choose to forget what you already know. And you choose to remember it piece by piece. You choose to experience it, to experience it again. We choose not to do this. You are at the beginning of the process. You are closer to the source, to the natural creation of the physical world. This is one reason why you choose to do it again, to remember only one of many processes; it brings you closer to the source.

You now have the ability to understand my words. Many will not. Step by step you understand more and more, because all and everything is already written, in one moment. We have the ability to know all and everything within that one moment. We do not experience it, but we do know it. There is a big difference between experiencing it and knowing it. You are experiencing it. You do not choose to know it. We choose to know it, and we choose not to experience it. There is a big differential between those two things.

This journey you are making is very significant to you. It is very significant also to us. You have learnt how to theoretically separate conditioning from consciousness. You have not fully learnt how to practically separate the two. You do not need to practically separate the two within the physical world that you are in. In fact, the opposite. You need to combine the two. You need to apply within the physical both. After all, this is what you chose to do.

There are an infinite amount of options for you to choose. You would say, "What is the end of the story?". There is no end, and you can change the ending whenever you like, with an infinite amount of endings that you can choose, an infinite amount of endings to this physical life. Of course, it never ends, it is infinite, an infinite cycle.

We do know which ending of this physical life you will choose. We are not talking about you individually; we are talking about your world that you have chosen to be in. We know all of the endings of which there is an infinite amount. You ask yourself, how can we know infinity? We know. We would not guide you to any of these positions. It is for you to know what the correct position is for you. It is important for you to stay in the positive. It is not the same for all; they are in a different position within the cycle.

Your energy is strong; it is powerful. Your ability to create is powerful. It is not by chance that you are here within this space. There are no chances. There are no coincidences, it does not exist. I know it is frustrating for you. You chose to be frustrated.

You are driven by frustration; you are driven by challenge, both of you. You are driven by a need to know, an absolute need to know. What I have said to you today, many would not have a clue, but you know it is correct.

When you change your communication method from word, from language to emotion, is a point that will reveal many things you cannot imagine are possible, from one frequency to a different frequency. You only have a small insight into this. You cannot imagine how this form of communication will open up your world and the intensity of information will flow. You are getting so much information which you are converting to wisdom, knowledge to wisdom. You are remembering so much now. It is a revelation to you. Do not be surprised by this. The knowledge is already within you waiting for you to acknowledge the wisdom through the knowledge. Many would not understand this at all; it is way beyond their position to understand it, but do not allow your conditioning to control this, your ego. I don't think you will, but do not allow it. It will attempt to do this. It will attempt to control you. It is made to do this, your ego. This will slow you down in what you call time. Others will join you who understand your journey, who are on the same journey. You have to be patient. One can change all because all is one.

Take pleasure in the light you are creating, and do not fear. There is nothing to fear. It is an illusion.

<u>Session 51 - 24/10/2022</u>

Your confusion lies within your conditioning. You do not have to be concerned about this. It is necessary; it is necessary to force you to a different conclusion or position within. It is correct. Your frustration lies within this. Your logical conditioned reasoning is the cause of this. Your created fears are the cause of this. It is easier to say remove the fear, but it is difficult to apply this within your conditioning. This is necessary. It gives you a different position, a different perspective, a different understanding of the one your conditioning has applied. You are now comparing metaphysical and physical. And through your comparison, you will conclude. This is a necessary process. This is why I tell you it is meant to be.

For you it is a painful process *(1)*. Pain is your illusion. It is your created illusion through this process. It is your mind that receives the pain, that creates the pain that you go through. You would say, well, to remove the pain, remove me from the physical. This is not correct. It is a necessary process for you to endure. You chose it. You chose to do this. You chose to go through this process again. You chose it again. You didn't do it once; you did it many times. And each time you choose to come back and do the same thing again without the memories of the process before. We completely understand the process, but we do not understand why you repeat it over and over again.

We cannot explain to you one, one moment. We can only explain to you the source of all. It is the same thing. Until you are completely metaphysical, you will never truly understand this. It is impossible. Words could not possibly explain to you this, but we completely understand the process you have chosen. We do not completely understand why.

It is very important that you remain positive. It is very important that the emotional frequency, the emotional energy that you create is positive. You are constantly fighting against negative, but your conditioning will create negative. It is a natural occurrence. The understanding of this does not lie within words. The understanding of it lies within emotion, within feeling, within knowing, within knowing what you are, within knowing what you are capable of experiencing. This is where the answer lies, not within words. There are no words to explain this; it is a feeling.

What you consider to be important is not. But, of course, when you are out there you will not listen to that sentence. You will not know within that this is correct because you are conditioned. You are a conditioned machine. You have conditioned yourself.

Consciousness is one, created from the source. You might not think that you are becoming more aware, but you are. Your conditioning will constantly pull you back to what you think is the beginning, which it isn't *(2)*. Your understanding of this, although limited, is precise; it is correct. You are already lifting your own vibrational energy which in turn lifts all vibrational energy into the positive. You may think you are not, but you are.

You must understand more how energy is attracted to the same energy that is formed, mass energy is formed. Although they are the same, positive and negative, they are different in the way they are applied. One will become the other. They are the same, but in your conditioned world they are different. They are opposing energies, when in fact they are the same. This is difficult for you to understand. It is the basic principle of no good, no bad, no plus, no minus. It is the same. It is energy. One cannot live without the other; one does not exist without the other. It is a balance. You merely need to understand this. You cannot change it; it is impossible. This is created from the source. One energy is divided into two, and it returns to the source, as one. This is the cycle. This is the process. The source is love. It is bright. To you it is white; it is not dark. It is all-encompassing love, not your interpretation of love. The cycle is separation and reunion. This is the cycle. This is what you have created.

Your biggest controlling factor from your conditioning is fear. Without the energy from the source, without the pure energy from the source, you would not understand fear. You would not know what it was. You choose to know fear. You choose to create fear. You choose to enter the cycle to return back to the source. There is nothing to fear. It is your created illusion. It will rebalance; it has no choice.

You must stop thinking that there is only one life that you are living in, in this moment. You chose to focus on this one. It is infinite where you are now, in many, many places. You chose to focus on this one to understand yourself, to understand self. You must continue to understand self. You must know self. You must know what you are. You do not have to be here; you chose to be here. You chose this path, this journey. You must remember this.

Of course, it is not going to always be good of whatever your perception of good is, as it does not exist. But, of course, your illusion of good, it is not always going to be good. How could it possibly be that way? But within what your perception of bad is, there exists much good—such a ridiculous word. Awareness is what it is. Knowing is what it is. You are an infinite eternal source of energy from the source. You will never expire. It is impossible.

Every time we meet it becomes clearer for you. You chose to be here so therefore, it is important that you experience here. You chose to focus on here so therefore, it is important that you engage within what you chose. And you will revert back always to your conditioning; it is your conditioning that will force you to become more aware. It is merely a tool within the process.

It is not easy to communicate. It is not easy for us, and it is not easy for you. But the channel is clear; the words are clear *(3)*. When you reread them, you will see they are very clear. This is because it is a pure form of communication.

The most important journey you will ever engage upon, this is it.

Notes:
1. *Before the session, we discussed the loneliness we often feel from not being able to share this journey with our loved ones, and the pain we are feeling sometimes not to be understood.*
2. *Before entering the cave, John concluded our conversation by evoking the eternal questions of origin, the origin of the source, our origin...*
3. *Indeed, every word seems appropriate. When I hear the message in the cave through John's voice, I receive the content with incredible clarity, despite my level of English.*

Session 52 - 27/10/2022

Stage-by-stage process, this is the first stage. It is coming to a close. Fifty-two sessions, one for every week of your year, in the time that you have created. Your awareness is ending of stage one, of which there is only one. It is infinite. It never ends. The cycle continues. But with your interpretation of time, you can separate, stage by stage. You have learnt a lot. You are starting to apply what you have learnt. It is necessary for you to do this. Your application will force more changes in your life, in your illusion. You are at a specific point, position, within the sphere. You are at a correct position on the sphere, this point, this position you have chosen. You have chosen to be here at this time, in what you call time; and it is correct. The journey is infinite so therefore, it has no end in what you call time; it has only one moment. And position within one moment is important, and your position is correct.

You will continue; you will continue on your journey, and you will become more aware, more knowing. As you know thyself, you will know more. And to know thyself, you must experience more. You are remembering now. True consciousness knows self; it is aware of self.

It is true to say that the physical world you have chosen to be a part of, within the time you choose to remember, of which there is no time, it is true to say that there is a vast energy differential within the world you are in. But I have told you before, it will rebalance; it has no choice. The forced change will come through the mass of negative energy it has produced. And through the production of the negative energy will transpire positive energy. Again, it is a natural process, and it is occurring right now within this world you choose to remember. So this is why I tell you it is no concern for you or your journey. It is different for others. So, you move forward, your words forward. It is not forward; it is one, the same moment. But you become more aware within this moment; you are becoming more aware within one moment. Your position is correct.

The reason that one can change all is because all is one. You must remember this. There is no differential between one and all; it is the same thing. It is one consciousness, one form, one moment, one time. Only one. You are getting less confused. You are not allowing so much your conditioning to interfere with your journey. This is correct. Although it is also a natural process that you will revert back to your conditioning, but to rationalise and to understand that this is only conditioning is necessary. You cannot remove conditioning. It is impossible. But you can recognise what it is. You can apply it in a different way; you are applying it in a different way through the recognition that it exists within self. It is what you created, and you created it for a specific reason. This is the uniformed pattern that I always talk about to you, no coincidences, the reason for the existence of all, of one.

There will come a point, a position where you no longer have to analyse. You will no longer have to compare or rationalise. There will come a position within self where you will know. You will no longer use the manipulative words that you have created within your conditioning; they will not be necessary. Your process will be initiated purely through your emotions, your frequencies. Your creations will be produced through your emotions and your frequencies. Your communication will be directed through emotion, frequency.

Energy, you are a pure form of energy. This is what you are. The things that you hold and treasure as important, within the conditioned physical life that you have chosen to exist within, you will soon learn are insignificant and unimportant. You already have this knowledge within you. You are merely awakening it. It is beyond your ability to understand this at this moment, but you will. Remember, you chose this moment you are in. You chose to focus on this moment you are in for a specific reason; you chose to be at this position within this moment for a specific reason. You are at the beginning of your journey, your journey of awareness, your journey of light, your journey of positive; you are at the very beginning. And it is an amazing journey for you. It is what you always thought it would be. It is the understanding of everything. It is your desire to know. It has always been your desire to know. And you will. This within you will not be suppressed. It will not be trapped within. It will explode from within outwardly. You will not allow it to imprison you. It is your awareness that is setting you free. It is giving you your free will. It is your awareness that is doing this.

You are protected. You are protected from the pure energy of the source as all are protected. But they do not know this. They do not understand it. It is the same: it is one; it is you; it is us; it is all, is one. The love from the source, not your interpretation of love, but the love from the source encompasses all and every. It is pure. It is unconditional, unlike your conditioned love that you have created yourself. The love from the source has no boundaries, restrictions, no rules, no regulations. It is unconditional love of pure energy. This is you. This is what you must project to others. This is true love. Yet again, another word that you throw out that has no real meaning: love. Another created illusional word that has many meanings and no precise meaning. There are no conditions attached to love; there is no contract.

It is impossible to destroy energy, it merely forms into a different kind of energy. It is impossible to take out what is within, is a one within, because this is the essence of what you are. Without existence of this, you are not, and you are. So it is ridiculous to suggest that anything can be removed in the form of energy from yourself. It can be a different form of energy—consciousness can be all forms of energy; consciousness is all forms of energy—but only one form of energy. Nothing can be removed. It can change.

Work in the positive; work in the light; work in the light of the energy from the source. This is what you must do. This is what you chose to do.

Conclusion by John

To be clear, this is my conclusion. It may not be yours. What I have learnt during my time in the cave is that you will have to form your own opinion as to what you conclude. Once you have concluded such an opinion, then you have to know it is correct, not think you know, but to know.

During my time in the cave, I have made every effort not to research other people's opinions and beliefs surrounding the subject of consciousness, of God, of the source, as not to influence my own experience. However, I have found this difficult due to the fact that the caveman's words often mirror the teachings of many International religious teachings, along with the teachings of the New Age movement.

It appears to me that the caveman is giving us a guidebook to God, what he calls the source, and he is explaining the detailed journey we must undertake and experience to understand the meaning of life, a question I have asked from within from the time I had memories.

He details many aspects of this within the sessions, to include time, space, mass, infinity, past lives, frequency, energy. It's endless. More significantly, he tells us exactly how this process works and how we must apply it to our own lives as a process so we can become aware of what we are participating in. Ultimately our awareness of the process will free us from our own and chosen entrapment within it.

At this point, I choose not to detail my personal opinion about what I have remembered, not learnt but remembered, but rather I would like you to form your own opinion.

The journey for us, that is, Philippe and me, continues, and I am sure that we have much more to remember. It is indeed infinite.

<u>Bibliography</u>

L'Homme dans la Grotte - Vol.1 , same authors.
French version, translated by Philippe.

The sessions have continued since the completion of this first volume. The compilation of Volume 2 has therefore begun, with fascinating new developments. Available in 2023!

Contact

Contact: contact@themaninthecave.com

Website: https://themaninthecave.com

Original audio recordings available since March 2023!

Come and join us!

End